HAIBUN DE LA SERNA

99 NEO-BARROCO HAIBUN

Also by Paul E. Nelson

American Sentences

A Time Before Slaughter/Pig War: & Other Songs of Cascadia

American Prophets (Interviews 1994-2012)

Organic in Cascadia: A Sequence of Energies

Anthologies co-edited:

Samthology

Make It True Meets Medusario

Make It True: Poetry From Cascadia

56 Days of August: Poetry Postcards

13 — APR — 2022

For Matthew —

w/ huge appreciation
for our work
together.

Haibun de la Serna

99 Neo-Barroco Haibun

Love —

Paul

PAUL E. NELSON

Goldfish Press, Seattle, Washington

For permission requests, write to us at the address below.

ISBN 13: 978-1950276-16-5
ISBN 10: 1-950276-16-3

Library of Congress Control Number 2021939222

Cover design by Amy McClure
Cover painting "Ode to Life" by William Turner

Goldfish Press is a literary press of all genres.

Goldfish Press
4545 42nd Ave. SW
Suite 211
Seattle, WA 98116

Website: goldfishbooks.com

Some of these poems were published previously in Hambone, as a Breadline broadside, Hoarse, Make it True: Poetry From Cascadia, Emerald Reflections, A Time Before Slaughter/Pig War: & Other Songs of Cascadia, Washington 129: Poets of Washington, Make it True meets Medusario, Sons & Daughters, other publications and the Capilano Review where one poem earned the Robin Blaser Award selected by George Bowering. Many of these haibun were written at different writing residencies and the author wishes to give thanks to the Helen Whiteley Center on San Juan Island, Washington, Doe Bay on Orcas Island, Washington, The Rainforest Hostel in Forks, Washington and the Lake in Loleta, California, coordinated by the Morris Graves Foundation, all of these places in Cascadia. Haibun #35 and 36 were written in China thanks to Denis Mair and Jidi Majia who gave me the opportunity to attend the Qinghai Lake International Poetry Festival. Gratitude to publisher Koon Woon, http://nowiknow. com/the-hobo-code/ for Hobo Code images and meanings. The author is also profoundly grateful to Amalio Madueño for the chapbook of a selection of early haibun, as well as for the kind (and intelligent) introduction, to the editing wizardry of Adelia MacWilliam, to José Kozer for opening up the world of the neo-barroco and Pablo Baler for tips on the neo-barroco approach to making the poem and the work of Ramón Gómez de la Serna respectively.

When you find your place where you are, practice occurs.

—Dōgen

Preface: The Poem As High Energy Construct

In this innovative series of poems Paul Nelson has combined contemporary neo-barroco poetic style inspired by José Kozer and Ramón de la Serna with a 17th century Japanese form eternalized by the poet Bashō, the most well-known early writer of the haibun tradition. Mixed with a soupçon of Ginsberg's "American Sentences" format and a profound grounding in Olson's Projective Verse poetics, the poems of Haibun de la Serna demonstrate an innovative combination of contemporary poetic styles and established poetic genres.

The poems, to quote the well-known Cuban poet José Kozer, "...have a density which is not excessive & ... bring forth intelligibility; there is a sense of flow and [I feel] the hand moving on the paper, the ink flowing naturally... As if it all flowed easy, which I know is not so, but felt as easy, going along, just flowing. Good modernity..."

Good modernity, indeed. Nelson's previous book of poems, A Time Before Slaughter, demonstrated this modernity in his ability to energize language in a focused look at the history and current affairs of the Puget Sound region.

Ramón G. de la Serna: Untranscendental Meditation

Nelson is inspired to this series of poems by the poems of Ramón Gómez de la Serna (1889-1963). De la Serna was known for "Greguerías" aphorisms that correspond to Ginsberg's American Sentences and traditional one-liners of comedy. Spain's chief exponent of avant-garde writing in the early 20th century, de la Serna established a famously influential literary tertulia at the centre of Madrid and produced some of the most original works in Spanish of the twentieth century — the existential-surrealist novel El hombre perdido [The Lost Man] (1947) and his extraordinary neo-baroque autobiography Automoribundia (Automoribund) [1948].

American Sentences

Allen Ginsberg created this form, to provide a uniquely American version of the Japanese haiku. Nelson has taken this form as a daily practice, writing one every day since January 1, 2001, and using it as a way to hone his own perception and spirituality. It is one way he's kept a journal of events in his life and the world while he sharpens his ability to capture a "snapshot of the moment" in a concise way.

Seventeen syllable sentences owe as much to the Buddhist side of the Beat movement as well as to de la Serna's own program. Like de la Serna, Nelson aims to divest himself of conventional consciousness so as to adopt a unique way of being in a society dominated by an industry-generated-culture. More than a rejection of that culture, it is among the first steps in "nation-building". Creating alternatives to large, out-dated centralized bureaucratic governments intent on perpetuating war consciousness with torture, endless violent occupations and attacks on the commons. Nelson sees them as Anarcho-leftist/bioregionalist/mammal patriotism chiseled out seventeen syllables at a time.

Open Form & Organic Poetry

The poems of Haibun de la Serna are grounded in uniquely 20th century poetics with roots in the Black Mountain School, Projective Verse and whose sources include W.C. Williams, Charles Olson, Joanne Kyger, Robert Duncan, Robin Blaser, Denise Levertov, Nathaniel Mackey and Michael McClure. Nelson is a proponent of the Organic approach to poetry and Open Form poetics. In concurrence with Ezra Pound, Nelson is convinced that it is the artist's job to be the antennae of the race in and to "prevent a culture from repeating the same dull round over again in the words of William Blake." Nelson espouses a "whole-systems, organismic, or process" view of reality which values intuition as much as rationality, and does not consider any element of a system irrelevant.

In his 2006 essay, Crafting the Organic Poem, Nelson discusses Canadian poetry's influence on Open Form poetics, and by extension, the poetry in this volume. Discussing the influence of British Columbia's George Bowering on Open Form poetics Nelson states: ". . . poets of the Open Form tradition became known, including Charles Olson and Robert Creeley . . . [through] their focus on Beat and Black Mountain literature, helping Vancouver to become a world nexus comparable to San Francisco for this stance-toward-poem-making as evidenced by the legendary 1963 Vancouver Poetry Conference. Bowering ... has demonstrated a knack for using the strategies of the Open to maintain the poem as high energy construct. . . In his book of essays on poetics. . . known as Craft Slices, Bowering states: "I do not compose poetry to show you what I have seen, but rather because I have seen. That is, this poet's job is not to tell you what it is like, but to make a poem…So the test of a poem is not in how it adheres to your experience (though that can be a pleasure too) but in how it coheres as something made. This is not to say that you can squash together any old thing and declare yourself pleased…the point is that you are adding something to the world, something that was not there before. If you have any good feelings about the world, you will want to add something that will not diminish it in quality." (Craft Slices 6).

In sum you will encounter in these pages something that was not there in the world before and that will add to it in quality.

Amalio Madueño
(Excerpted from the 2001 chapbook published by Ranchos Press, New Mexico)

Contents

99 Neo-Barroco Haibun

1. The Pigeon's Key

At dusk a homing pigeon flies overhead with a key to lock up the day.

—Ramón Gomez de la Serna

On Orcas it's a red tailed hawk lost in the steam from hot springs always finds its way over Otter Cove unless there's trouble. Blue Heron waits to push the world away, still, stands in the in-coming tide aware of the angel's sword aware the poison in the yew tree where power comes from evergreen from elder is anima. (Eihwaz holds the entire futhark.) In the dream we teach poetry in the former factory made of red brick and the glue of destitute kundalini. We're suspicious of their religion & the latihan's already worked its celestial shudder. The pigeon still there still aflight's full of donated wonder bread, flies north 'til it becomes one with an obsolete constellation. That's the key. Just ask the Sacred Kingfisher. Or is it belted?

Odin's sister
not his sister
hides in the yew's roots.

8:09A – 11.27.10
Doe Bay

1

2. Duende's Dancestep

Death is inaudible: in the intimacy of the house it walks on tiptoe.

—Ramón Gomez de la Serna

Skulks adjacent to the seaside Orcas November mountain hoping to garnish a wave with a tendon or femur, anyplace can morph into Slaughter, even a rocky vista redolent with pines, firs and rose hips drop onto soft moss next to deer scat. Handholds. The shadow lying *beneath my copy of eternity* to glimpse the blonde lock of yours somehow noticed when late November afternoon sun hits a certain angle of my shoulder. (My morning shudder.) Beyond Obstruction, beyond the demonic realm of parlor tricks to near where waves of the incoming tide rebound off an off-island rock (an island itself) to make concentric semi-circles in a futile path back to Fidalgo. They'll die en route as you and I might struggling for that last glimpse that last lover's smiling eyes that death-bedside daughter who eases the track back to the garden.

Cliffgrip measured, all
senses acute but who
studies surrender?

6:02P – 11.27.10
Doe Bay

3. Quickening

Time is closer to dust in libraries.

—Ramón Gomez de la Serna

Inside the dust, universes with their own constellations, some obsolete, all gain velocity a planet in need of periodic leap seconds when the ancient light from stars gathered, careened around hallucinated Olympic firs causing alarm. Fire emanating snakes. Quickening can be an apocalypse or a birthcrisis can be a fetus or a species. *The word "quick" originally meant "alive".* Whitehead called the present the *vivid fringe of memory tinged with anticipation.* Another occasion's what you make of it, how you justify. Ringed with wintering scotch broom or the pods left behind by lavender blossoms (ones he might've crumpled in the minute universes of his sweater pocket) & she goes from zero-to-car driving in sixty seconds to give him the gift of the present, saw his history laid out in microscopic skin flecks she wipes from library shelves beyond the photo of his father, still alive, still holding that pipe, posing. You can almost smell the Walgreens cheap tobacco you were to teenage shoplift later, time as cloud & ash & the exile of attempted compassion rebounds as a flaming email but that don't stop you from reaching out to the higher selves.

> Constellations may be patient
> but they won't wait
> for the end of your hallucination.

9:42A – 11.28.10
Doe Bay

3

4. Angel Hack

Never forget that it was an angel that invented swords.

—Ramón Gomez de la Serna

Never forget it is the oldest Bodhisattva carries one aflame in his right hand to carve a slice off duality. Never forget a sword's a scalpel can hack at nafsu, that which fosters soul erasure, hack at the snag that stifles your hike up Entrance Mountain, hack to clear a path as King Solomon might machete as mere threat to find a way into co-mercy. Nature sometimes needs a knife now & again, give gristle to the dog, liberate axis & om-fire or simply to slice up the mango. You might like pastelitos de guayaba. You might be sickened by what antepasados are urging you to cut just this side of Obstruction or may be Frank Morgan alto-honking the daylight out of front row yuppies in full babble, George Cables right behind him as he was with Art Pepper on the prison tune, The Trip. *Why did they chop off the missionaries heads* the child asked, but they were no mere visitors, only the first line of colonialists whose angels have no swords whose single god has a beard and vendetta, whose trick is stealing fire, whose exceptional American time is running out.

> Rocket's red glare.
> Colors don't run but burn
> sliced by Manjushri's flaming saber.

8:34A – 11.29.10
Doe Bay

4

5. Carbonism

A carbon copy is taken of everything that is said in the dark.

—Ramón Gomez de la Serna

A diamond reflects all darkness whispered in a room lit by faint beams from the Cold Moon. The moon when Horns are Broken Off. A long night's Oak Moon almost seen dodging sunbeams, applying mascara, ordering another foamy cappuccino. A diamond's a girl's confidant & the hardest allotrope of carbon. Buckyball's a carbon (C60) but I've never had one festooning an earlobe or translating Miles' *Mademoiselle Mabry* from wax into the darkness of sound's primitive hunger. Copy this: photo of the goats return after dark to an always older city. Energy lines still flow out footsteps made by the swarming invisible dead of Sealth's tribe, beyond silence of the pathless woods climb up any Entrance Mountain. A carbon copy being taken by shades at the malwort, @ the indy neighborhood coffee house where the proprietor builds community one sneer at a time @ the bathhouse by Lake Xacuabš. A carbon copy of everything said in the dark, every grunt and mastication, sometimes trading phosphorous for arsenic, entrails for a larger heart, evidence of a 27th Genesis on a planet in need of at least one more.

Absence of reflected light
(or) photon storehouse
for the footsteps of one more
invisible tribe.

10:56A – 12.2.10
Sbux, 212th & W Valley

5

6. Echoes (After Nate Mackey)

The Last Trumpet is the echo of the echo of the repeated echo of the First Trumpet.

—Ramón Gomez de la Serna

As an undertone or overtone, overlord or undertaker. When stuck can become strict stricken or structure. The last trumpet could be the diamond scratching out stuck sound's primitive hunger or the antepasados' disembodied wail translated to alto squawk or hawk's circular trail this side of constellations (obsolete or not so) a nutrient manifesting as enthusiasm or arsenic in the place of phosphorus, the alchemist burning his own piss to find gold or a similar lost essence. The echo finds its own place in the canyon rock, funds its own defense from soul erasure, fumbles for safety in the fronds of the sword fern a previous angel must have left there before conifers, before cedar's relocation after glaciers & a song that would have made it so. Or maybe the echo found its way into cliffside blueberries warmed by September afternoon sun or in the petals of the Indian Paintbrush (Prairie Fire) as a hairwash or toxic condiment replacing the sulfur with selenium. The first trumpet echoes a sound that became a song & a song that lifted grace out of the muscles of angels into ligaments & sinew that saw the race it was in to beat the echo back before the ripples of water could recede, again, in September, when school resumes. Echo as salient reminder, the angle always pointing inwards, the innards ready to be splayed on any good day to die the collection of Obstruction rocks reminds us.

A Resolution recedes
Coltrane tells us
but some echo is always
a life.

3:16P – 12.10.10

7. Winter Solstice Lunar Eclipse *(For Sam Hamill)*

In Paris the winter sun is an omelette which arrives cold.

—Ramón Gomez de la Serna

In Seattle winter moon's barely visible through solstice eclipse-impairing clouds (stratocumulus) 'til we crash & don't spy the darkest night in centuries though it too's bonecold. Arrives as the eye of a Puyallup organic carrot candied by Tahoma volcanic ash or a murder of crows bare tree shelter'd above the Ferdinand treehouse. A night of no moon. A Long Night's Moon. The longest night's moon enables global brightening set off by bug bombs & other aerosolismo.
The Seattle Long Night's Winter Moon enables solstice celebration, respite from mist & veiled mass of droplets a only a nephologist could love & all that's behind every mal de ojo: Coyote's skulk, the hallway Mexican cat standoff, the movie camera cocked at the side of the skull, often somewhere deeper than we can spy. A Winter Solstice Lunar Eclipse not since Galileo was living out his days under house arrest, his day's Assange, *full moon on steroids*, always an apocalypse for someone else.

> After collecting stents, Sam's
> liver won't stand his heart
> operation, darken'd by a AWOL
> Long Night's Moon.

The Long Night's Winter Moon's eclipse's free to skate another four score & four years here's a towel you can toss, here's an earthquake nails 200K Haitians into makeshift coffins, or a thousand Chileans. Arrives as toxic Moscow air & the flight north of several more forests with 62,000 sq mi. of new riceland in Pakistan 18 countries w/ their hottest day ever.
Oh Sam.
Don't start quoting Li Po to us. Don't let Lorazapam get the best of yr Zen. Don't take that Kevorkian treatment. The Long Night's Missing Winter Solstice Moon's an illusion. It's there as much as compassion & a move into the ancient belt of old starfires surging our way. Sam, spy the terrier. She don't seem too nervous & the links prefer your laugh to the scattering of your ashes.

10:55A – 12.22.10

8. Ain't No Gusano

Ever since men started to travel by underground they have begun to lose their fear of death: they have already become familiar with the worms.

—Ramón Gomez de la Serna

Could be he was chthonic, so close to Olympus, Asklepius cut out of his mother's womb still hangs on to that snake, still one of 88 keys played by the night sky, still living off occasional lungful of interstellar oxygen, a Greek bearing the gesture of gift snakes, how many in such a hurry to get to 6 Underground Street, who can call out the daughter of swords, can cut away the lunge & the castings.

In need of a lightning strike fuses silica sand into glass channels, rearrange office chairs in a lost tower, a bony hand reaches out the sea for one of seven empty cups, no song a deity would have you sing of sparks of light shot from his ever white teeth, the bloodied eye still leaks salt, elders animate every step & syllable. This ain't no gusano steppin' out with a Cuban slide.

After his last solo
the trumpeter opens the spit valve
out comes blood.

Outcome blood and Miles knew it, cued up & shot into a corner pocket like a bloodstone he might've found on a beach near Obstruction. (Heliotrope). Tried to reel it in but his scream didn't attract a single echo. Underground he don't move so fast. Underground Kuan Yin'd find it hard to hear the grief moans or distinguish 'em from coyote howls. Underground find yourself with much more company than you might've thought but those ain't smiles on their faces just the first hint of what went wrong.

10:28P – 1.2.11

9. Ancestor (Dream) Dirt

It was one of those days when the wind was trying to speak.

—Ramón Gomez de la Serna

The Aranda word for dream also means ancestor, so the poet says. So the poet sews as if a right to the ear that floored him in Jersey, or the Binghamton wine bottle that opened up new realms of self; stars for a would-be vigilante blood trickled forehead tricked by coyote in a fedora. The poet continues with *rasp is a recursive form, a net of echoes; it catches*, it repeats, reverberates in slightly similar frequencies, too many messages no god has any time to damn.

> History is nightmare
>   gnostics might say. The night
> wind brings with it one
>   invisible worm.

Burrows into ancestor dirt w/ a mind of its own. Electrolytes in the Kansas ancestor dirt the color of fossils. Ancestors waking you from a dream in which bullet holes in the head foretell attempted Arizona assassinations the worm burrows into his bed of crimson joy which just happens to be the head of a not-so-innocent bystander, the elders drunk on palm wine or single malt scotch into which restless dead've crept to rig a marriage without one single shotgun. Dirt in the lavender blossoms with a mind to festoon city sidewalks few walk no more. Dirt with a sense of humor yearning to be a nurse log made of cedar, waiting (wanting) to soften a daydream 'n echo an earlier commune of poetry. There's a gunfight in church, then someone's a mind to turn the garage into dirt, then the dreamer awakes, finds no worm, only an itch & itches to return to the terror only night (or history) can bring.

11:36P – 1.8.11

9

10. Rivers

Rivers do not know their names

— Ramón Gomez de la Serna

& learn to live in dirt, find their ancient way via the magnetosphere (an autonomic nervous system) the medium of 5,000 red wing blackbirds dead where radar picked up a *non-precipitation target* or 5,000 more dead in Pointe Coupee Parish a fur piece from the makeshift graveyard of Gary Ridgway & his ligature maneuvers robbed the Green of some of its shimmer prophets know is under river gods made from mud.

When to call Duwamish *Duwamish* when the Black is murdered? When White or Green? Follow Green back east to Stampede Pass, up beyond Weston, Lester, the Hot Springs, Nagrom, Maywood, Humphreys, Eagle Gorge, Lemolo, and Kanaskat itself named after a chief whose heart was wicked toward Bostons & whose musket might have put the final ball into Slaughter.

When turn attention to silver rivers beyond the Van Allen Belt & plasmasphere? Even the 100,000 dead Arkansas fish know the Tampa runway's just a little off & a pole shift much overdue. We all seek refugium more than just a mountain range w/ peaks higher   than the tops of where glaciers were.   Refugium from a culture crafted in a lab dedicated to the torture of all living things everywhere, learning gets turned on its skull and we just want to stay above the Green's last fatal meander.

A river may not know its name
but call it Staq,
White,
Green or Duwamish &
it may share its heartbeat
or starshimmer.

12:23P – 1.24.11

10

11. Charioteering

Her old hands grip life like a bird's claws on a branch.

—Ramón Gomez de la Serna

A branch of the family tree succumbed to aggregates (skandhas) *giddy-up*
they say & modern-day gladiators plunge a knife in the side of the horses
of instruction, *make this chariot go!* But it can only be a pile of faint traces,
bookmarks, tweets, tantalum (not the homeopath's sulfur) for which we'd
devour the lion's last habitat and fund the latest land & culture-rape.

Bird-grip, not the Bloodhawk's foveal vision, a laugh for the Apocalypse, a
shudder of grey, buff and brown plumage, antidote to the Kingfisher's flash
& machine-gun mambo as Manjushri might advise, compassion & freedom
from delusion where the Bloodhawk vision comes in, wipe the stars off
your boots in a vigil we pretend is no vigil.

Bird-grip addicted
to meaning, shades beyond the reason of meat and surrender, the streams
stretching into shadows of memories made us fully here, revering only the
moment and its glaciers feeding Lake Xacuabš – their perennial shudder
shoving off the adolescents. She grips the chariot reins 'til fingernails draw
palm wine, 'til the panic in the eyes of forest horses spreads to fill the sky,
Bloodhawk's paradise. Gold and brown eyes date to the Eocene, the bird-
grip much, much older.

How we all thought refugia
much more complex than
letting the reigns (reins) rains
go

6:25P – 1.26.11
@ SPLAB

11

12. Stag Party

The stag is the son of tree and lightning.

—Ramón Gomez de la Serna

A statue, not a statue, still wary of unarmed humans, still able to bolt over the forest's green galaxies, still able to make a meal of last night's camp urine-flavored dirt. Making less sound than the raven cackle atop the Doug Fir, less than the boot crunch on snow melt, less that the rhododendron leaf shaking in the January Breitenbush sun.

The stag awaits a beard, knows no master but morning velocity, stalks unguarded Port Townsend gardens fleeing, as we all should, hungry Chimicumians. Leaves comet trails that settle as moss in the Cascade forest. Signals via silence and leg twitches to the chief of the Bird Tribe & to the man with the wry smile, flaming hat and penchant for hairfish.

The stag's a sentry for Zeus, Thor's pet, reminds us of the animal self we left behind for hamburgers, traffic cameras and cappuccino. How the hunger creates elaborate castles of war & hierarchy, napalm & waterboards & of the day, post-apocalypse, when we might trade blood for tree sap, ears for an outstretched madrone branch, eyes for the Blood Hawk's foveal vision that can spot squirrels & Andromeda from light years above the plain.

2:05P – 1.30.11
@ Breitenbush

13. Free Egypt

We should put a mark on the sky to see how quickly the cathedral has been growing.

—Ramón Gomez de la Serna

We put the mark of mammal revolt on the sky above Tahrir square where flame's a mark of celebration foreheads touch their patch of holy ground in unison, all holy, a dictator's flight power protection of la raza, of Algiz the buck's antlers & Aljazeera making every despot's move an international incident Aquila making everything else moot. *Tools with which to construct narratives.* Meat w/ which to construct memories of inhalation (the ageless narcotic of freedom) stolen from a dictator in the shadow of a sphinx part limestone woman part indigenous cat.

A mark on the sky where cries of food riots leapt, hunger as organizing force, maybe this industrial ag thing ain't what it's cracked up to be, cracked a mark onto the sky above & on the dirt below where foreheads rest in surrender. The crack of a dictator's mouth (a smile) power the ultimate inebriate panic in a President's private eye that spreads to fill the sky & whiten his hair in *Nazi America* where we post pictures of our food on Facebook and think an immolation protest another chapter in the endless entertainment, forget the sacrifices of constellations of ancestors, squander our one meat moment on a casino or sitcom while this Turtle dreams of its own coups & Mayan prophecy stares us in the collective face glint of diamond in its smiling eye preparing to lift the last veil.

All dictators & corporate puppets will be made to dance from a casket of fire while celebration's an unmistakable blur we watch from behind the veil of a culture invented by henchmen & those who never know the sweet shudder of surrender. How the shoulders rumble, give way to a force lighter than meat, the animating principle, what makes the flight of the bloodhawk so simple & gives Aquila star force.

Shudder of another kind
Swiss banks freeze Egyptian assets.
Let them eat soup.

9:29A – 2.12.11
Vancouver

14. Mango Infloresence

A long wait in a bar: initials made with toothpicks.

—Ramón Gomez de la Serna

A short time to prepare morning duties. The mango does not get its due diligence. The peel will be cut off like science starting near the button & working in a spiral one hopes to not break. From there only a few snips of stubborn peel & hunks unfettered by the hairy &/or fibrous seed. How can one pass up at least a hunk or two even when in smoothie mode? I would not want it pickled as its Wikipedia entry suggests it was when transported to 17th century colonies in the Americas, but love the phrase found there *Mango inflorescence*. Could describe my state was after putting a hunk or two in my mouth for a too-brief moment before I realized I would not be able to save all the fruit from the holy seed.

No initials left in the peel tossed without ceremony into the square green compost bucket. None in the just washed dish pile, nor in forests of cat hair I find in the grooves next to the trim. But my traces are everywhere & mingle with yours. Most of the mango goes in the blender with the bananas you rejected and the soy milk you did not finish. Dishes dry much more quickly than I would have ever guessed, the smoothie goes down quick & the cats sleep.

Mango science
chew every last bit of flesh
let juice drip down every chin.

2:04P – 2.19.11
SPLAB

15. Tongues & Mirrors

All the mirrors of the past flow by, drowned in a river.

—Ramón Gomez de la Serna

Seen in eyeballs of dogfish plucked out by seagulls upon their spring return navigate a Stuck flow past broken Medicine Creek treaties past the last of lodgepole pines headed north to one of a few last refugia, past Oak Moons, volcanic ash & the routes lahars left. Bobbing past the Labrador with an eye on the prized stick past Miller cans thrown by Assman headed to Jakarta by way of stars & currents past the eyes of Siddartha recounting every encounter every face of every last love every fist & a few of the lost river gods, offerings to impermanence made in Stuck River mud, grass-haired, stone-toothed & eyed. Seen, eyes closed, in the rush of violet & heart-chakra green or some hallucinatory variant on a theme of letters dropped out the womb of the great mother. LETTERS which rise to form hawks of blood, dogfish & half-dog/half man creatures *high on the drugs of our glands*, letters fall from the belt of Orion or from the hunter's shoulder another runaway star afraid of stopping.

Here another mirror bobs, another cycle completes, how Hummingbirds reject the flock & yet form a sangha or rebellion in the hills, how they're (we're) all connected by tongues Kihlguulins displayed, how the woman fucked the bear prince & bore cubs how Nanasimget, his wife, & the Killer Whale kidnapper, how Sea Wolf eats three whales a day, Dogfish Woman & her mythic pups & Eagle Prince all connected by tongues, by blood, by the force that would run off a star, by first fields & voice, by interstellar imprimatur & longing & for the amusement of the Empress.

Mirrors bob in the river
so many jewels in her net

& yet all that unemployed skin.

10:55P – 3.2.11

16. Suicide Flowers

Beyond the tracks of the railway grow Suicide Flowers.

—Ramón Gomez de la Serna

And they could not wait to run with the camels in Egypt or seek retreat in an Igbo refugia or even its song HEY LA LA CU LA YA, cd not escape a Heart Shaped Box always with a need for a new complaint, not the pliant vision of a certain goddess, sinew's role in manifesting mammal reason free from rules made in that terror lab we mentioned last time. How the iron horse & all its dicks wd cut hobos in half, display their splayed entrails short of the refugia of the cat face of the kindhearted woman or the moon face of *Doctor Here Won't Charge.*

HEY LA LA CU LA YA
next to box cars & box cars & box cars, next to cases of red corn syrup masquerading as licorice sticks, no clarinets in sight, just the feeling of fight pummeled out of each crocus before their spring, each fireweed not yet ready to snow the Olympic sky at the next September breeze, the next blue gentian in a blueberry masquerade the villagers rally around chanting what bubbles up from the mothertongue as an intelligence of its own, free of the reach of heartmind, more a starforce reckoning with the latest satanic deviances be they Guantanamos or mortgages, Abu Ghraibs or student loans formed in the shape of a noose or another ligature maneuver.

A blossoming of madrones or Indian Paintbrush cut short by the demands of endless violent occupations never privy to the meat's own violet & fluorescent green smoke clouds billowing personal cartoons as the mind becomes the body's need for reason, but meat reason decides for itself the authenticity of every twist & hand clap, every chant to Allah, Jesu Christo or Massey experienced as one long vowel. Massey. Massey. Mercy.

> Rest in peace Kurt Cobain.
> We'll carve the park bench and
> resist with all our meat
> the man who sold the world.

KIND LADY
LIVES HERE

9:26A – 3.3.11

DOCTOR HERE,
WON'T CHARGE

17. Black Sounds

In order to remain quite alone, we should have to take off our selves.

—Ramón Gomez de la Serna

Roll up our sleeves. Revisit our cells. *Time and I against any two* she said &
the song that croaked out her throat was cracked, was *cante moro* he said, *cante
jondo* in a hinge paracritical in a lunge desperate. The black sounds trading
eigths & beyond. Walking the tightwire between ice & burn, between the
stars' explosion as climate-changed raindrops on the sidewalk before the
seven. (7).

Here (hear) a fathertongue dip into a bass clarinet
pull out a Green Dolphin Street or a veiled homage to the black sounds
of Velvet Fred Anderson viva! Here, trouble. The voice is cracked & the
getback gone forever. Hear the spirits gulped to activate another order: b
roken, problematic, eloquent. Duende awakened *in the remotest mansions in
the blood* & awake it must. In Madison and Cairo. In Tunis through the Sea
Gate, they cut off the arm of the Secret Police. Cante moro. Hear (here) the
black sounds growl louder. Johnny Griffin took a farm in France to make
his growl louder. Make lavender out of cracker attack dogs. Make mind &
meat a more latent shape.

How wartime calls us to *love
the rim of the wound* while fending off the henchmen. Pick off the corporate
scab, sleep under his bed. Make time for birdsong & marvel at crows.
Crow cackle the language for a state of crisis. Duende. The black sounds
congregate around the side door. The cymbals see, seek their summer hiss.
Like Lorca, lying there, still seeks to darken the sky. Open the wound.
Sudden shudder uncontrolled & a cracking of the song problematic. A dead
man in Africa's more alive than most men here in the land of the freaks of
nature. Darkened, as in a vigil most don't see. Duende. (Remember) The
getback gone & left with a blowback of wind & record weather. *Time and
I against any two* she said. The slow feeling of a live planet awakening to
ward off mammals in some kind of narcotic slumber. Scott Walker. Dick
Cheney. Rick Snyder. Peter King. White men in crisis fearing the lunge
of Malcolm, the chickens returning for roost. A white privilege gone the
way of duende.

Hear the black cat's throaty moan.
It's melody you remember
    when yr wayback
            with the worms.

THERE ARE
THIEVES ABOUT

THIS IS NOT
A SAFE PLACE

8:58A – 3.10.11

18. Noosphere Wormride

Among the special suitcases one has to buy for air travel, one should be made to carry the fear.

—Ramón Gomez de la Serna

Fear as form, measured out foot at a time not unlike the severed feet washing up on B.C. beaches, not the proportionlessness he sd more interested in shape and the light radiating out March crocuses the boy marvels at; light radiates from the blossoming cherry tree & its hummingbird armada dead serious about the hunt; light like the Buddha's *clear mirror reflecting images according to their forms from the field of blessings.* Starparts. The poem less a recipe and more the salient of Crick's edgeless biology & the light therefore shot off from. Form

                    as fabrication. March sunlight made the heat rise up, the feet wash up, the daffodils stiffen the stellar jay crack a staccato Wednesday wake-up call not unlike the light from a bell ring brings this assembly to order. Starts the sacred shudder. Wakes from the warmth of the cat-lined bed. Wants nothing but boundlessness to imagine wormride outside the crimson joy of the skull on the waves of the silver rivers of the noosphere toward maximum organized complexity be it Adrian the Chicago coyote ordering tunamelt at Quizno's or that of the nerves take over as the synapses engage in randomized neural activity when the warmth of divinity seeps in. *These virtues and merits cannot be measured* he said saying what the Buddhas of ten directions together could not fully expound.

                  Mente pura, as
         in the blue of a certain Seattle March
           sky

             sometimes & the faint light still leaks out of Blake's obsolete constellations, wormridden & impeccable. Make their own form their own cometflight from fear into proportionlessness a systemless system he insists. Spaceship Earth as shared vehicle. Gnostic porthole as danced by the naked happy genius of the household. Householder as supreme achievement where woodchop & watercarry's translated to freelance & dishwash. Dried carrot a trick turd in the catbox. Tending the fire & shimmer of every jewel in the net.

HOLD YOUR
TONGUE

THE SKY
is the LIMIT

9:46A – 3.23.11

20

19. Bendigas de Bloodhawk

Your heart cannot be deaf, because the telephones of the arteries keep it informed of what is going on.

—Ramón Gomez de la Serna

Form as cellular phone, phone as vast net of fat white cells, indeed – chain-link code-snippets salient as the broken river's mindful wander not unlike the lip loop the Bloodhawk studies bendigas indeed. Pre-preconditions & co-extensive with the reality as wily as magnolia blossoms & the rest of the verdant cosmos.

Form as proportionlessness the shape of every late March cherry blossom & angels getting fat on light. S?ayahus getting fat on everything else god bless my choked up mouth. River parts & mudbanks the child might've played in, playing you for a father, making grass-haired gods with stone eyes underneath the yoga windows opened by suicides in the darkest dungeons of slaughter.

Here he's traded November wind for crow's feet, a direct connection to a deep source flowing skullward (Allah's afterword) chanting fervent for an apocalyptic burn, the meat of the Olympics making spiritual muscle out of memory, milk out of proportionlessness, chants & shudders out of thusness. Butter from mud. Breath from teenage machismo. Blood as form & how brothers of different mothers find each other, from the one mother they recognize by the silver reflections off Bloodhawk's talons & her wily turquoise gleameyed smile.

Magnolia's March semaphore –
blossom-laden branches just this side of
skyscrapers & surging cities
of moss.

3:34P – 3.25.11

21

20. Gardenspace & Hawktime

When the blackbird flies away, it is as though the garden's shade is escaping.

—Ramón Gomez de la Serna

Air is the space in which time's blackgreen flow commences – the blackbird only one shade inhabiting the April skEba'kst-side garden. Without proportion is this jewel on this almost re-run of a cloudy Monday in the year of moss. In this year of endless magnolia blossoms, daffodils & hawks of all kinds, the garden's guardian. He who wd battle S?ayahus, he who would be the arbiter of space & shake the last cherry blossom free before the last April wind cd, he who finds fascination in how form evolves to meat the moment's shape as it's revealed note by note. All the oooooooo's ahhhh'd at. All the eeeeeeee's even. *AH* Allen'd say & he meant it just as the planet means war when the plate's rumbled reminder shows Cascadia's edge a gaian mal de ojo indeed

or maybe a wink similar to the kitten's leap (the only eye-weep necessary's that which reveals the thin mirror between self and Self) blackbird as messenger, Blackhawk as memoirist, the size of 18th century American cities coloring the eyes of rivals (Keokuk). All in the proportionless April skEba'kst-side garden. All when the crow flies revealing the garden's tendons which underlie its meat. All in eagle sight from above the Jose Rizal Bridge reflection banking off skyscraping maneuvers the Duwamish River just too polluted to see. All as real as clouds of hovering starlings, real as the eagle beak that snacks on heron eggs revealing the apocalyptic screech. Real as the monsoon's *striped triton tongue* and the reflection stealing land in treaties named after Medicine.

La lengua
goes two ways. One's either subtext
or doublespeak.

10:50A – 4.25.11

21. Fog Drip (The Age of Veil Lifting)

The fog was so thick that after it passed we found it rubbed out all the shop signs.

—Ramón Gomez de la Serna

& it comes in the age of veil lifting thicker than fists reinvents velocity /shows its universal solvent side. Past Willits & gateway set by Sequoia Sempervirens where *Welcome to Cascadia* signs are readied by itinerant wood lovers who masquerade as aging hippies saving the Eel River.

Fog reveals the age of veil removal, up it lifts beyond countries run by vegetables w/ aquarium-pump hearts, their shoddy war scholarship & their endless C student violent foreign occupations. (Gather seeds & Sequoia seed cones. Sip fogdrip & celebrate rainfall 100 inches & more.)

Velocity, the last drug in the age of fog. Velocity shaped & cultivated by would-be gardeners addicted to palmscreens. We, too, *sprout from dormant or adventitious buds at/or under the surface of the bark*, but mark it rebellion, or the reason initiated by ligaments & move me north (follow the fog.)

Nod to the *river god in love w/ his dreams* then, up river, Upp, Decamp, Longvale, Farley, Tatu, Dos Rios, surely we'd have seen these names speed by in dreams. Indian Spring, Woodman, Card Place, Nashmead. (Surely DeAngulo had a paddle, a gut hunch & a message for Fox and the waxing moon.) Reyes Place, Dunlap Place, Jim Leggett Place, Spyrock. Towns of the great fog aiding the work of the veil; antidote to the velocity of everlasting slaughter; a bloodhawk learns to circle, forests get out of town before a pole shifts (or after). I learn to sing my own body electric, remember breath lessons, envision endurance of trail-side blueberries warmed by eternal September sun, never run, keep the elder's voices alive in one's head *because one of us will die* he no longer will sing, but the orchid flower lives.

Here the nightmare may be
the hand that touched you
now colder than the rainrainrain.

10:53A – 5.13.11

22. Flag Drop
(After Gary Snyder and Han Shan)

Flags are the only ones to say goodbye to the clouds.

—Ramón Gomez de la Serna

The mountains and rivers are destroyed,
but the State survives

—Nanao Sakaki paraphrasing Tu Fu

The road through Stevens Pass takes you through Index, Startup, Sultan and past many huge backyard American flags, *haven't been for thirty years* Sam says after the age of espresso carts, espresso huts, mini espresso strip clubs and endless violent missions accomplished. A path, but no sign of a horse nor even a mythic one pulling a sun (what sun?) across a bronze age sky. Gorges meet just beyond Highway 2 beyond craggy peaks she can't capture through car windows, dew-bent grasses remember the July sun and hillside lodgepole pines hum/wait for immolation that surely will come. I've always been a sucker for shortcuts. My body asks of my shadow: *How can I outrun you?*

At the edge of a cliff, I chose a path *more alive than I ought to be.* There's Boulder Creek watershed below & bearpaths, raven's whooshing wingbeats, but who's satisfied with trails? Surely there's a shortcut around here & who knows what lies beyond the waytrail? White clouds cling to rocks til the fingernails draw wine & now I've lived here – what 22 years? Another spring and more magnolia blossoms drummed into dust by car tires. Lilacs festoon the city of poets & here winter's never too far away. Go tell families with flat screens and hybrids *What's the appeal of noise and bloodmoney?*

On Dirtyface Peak, it's cold. Not just this year, but ever since it thrust up there last time we acted this way. Jagged scraps keep the ice in icicle creek (*na-sik-elt*) cold as toes in Josephine Lake, they spit mist at Sitka Willows, Ponderosa Pines, Pacific Red Fir, Rocky Mountain Juniper & Pacific Dogwood opening up late May (& later) grass sprouting at June's end & no complaints from them about the short season. And here we are, in the mountains, eyes peeled like a bloodhawk's for the next poem. It may very well show up.

Gun my '01 civic through the future ghost towns where blackberry bushes bide time 'til supper. The jingoism sours my gut/smells like a fresh tomb. My shadow's not too far from here, in eyeshot of a box made of pine, ready for its own ashtray, but not my jiwa's final rest stop. Only the mindseye sees those ordinary bones, imagines the space in the skull where laughing teeth once were. In the hard drives of the Immortals they are purgatoried in namelessness.

You salute the flag – I'll
find a cold mountain stream
to drink up my   puny   dawn   song.

5:22P – 5.21.11
Leavenworth, WA

25

23. Seventh Breath
(After Gary Snyder and Han Shan)

Eternity envies us mortals.

—Ramón Gomez de la Serna

Promised her I'd stay in Slaughter til she prepared her flight. Near the banks of Lake Xacuabš'd work, cedars & pines catch rain/sway under the Scraping Moon. Moon of diminished crows who got *outta my yard* one clear May day. (So loud.) They say keep your ears peeled & the sound gets better. Under it the man's gray beard mumbles into a cellphone or the fog. He could be reciting Snyder or Dickinson to the five directions. Saturn's been around the sun once since I left home and have almost forgotten (like an Ivan Osokin) how I got here.

They want to know the way to Cat Peak, Dirtyface Peak, Mt. Olympus, Desolation: there's a through trail but takes a seventh breath. Ice is melting like a motherfucker & it ain't 'til May that sun rises & blurs in swirling fog. *How did I make it?* We don't yet share a heart, but when we do, you'll feel those palpitations freed by the end game of joy right here.

Settled in Cascadia decades ago & the projects just now start to sprout out cinco direcciones feels like lifetimes thanks to velocity, failed raptures & a state of perdido. You prowl backyards remembering dogwoods & lilacs, remember how to breathe watching things watch themselves. When you get this far into the mountains, clouds charged with sunlight pour over the cliffs and expire. An Indian mattress serves for a nap with blue sky blanket. Happy with dirt as heaven goes about its earth changes.

Still wonder
how close the rescue copter would've come
to the snowwrit S.O.S.

10:29P – 5.23.11

24. Dogwood Blossoms

When the hammer's head flies off, the nails laugh.

—Ramón Gomez de la Serna

Clamber up the Subud House steps, the trail goes on & on but inside. The gutter choked w/ oak leaves serves as cupboard for crow's crusts or crackers, the thin creek long underground, the park grass wet from rain in the spring of no spring. Cedar's song silent here, except when the wind stops maybe we can hear its sap run. Who can bound the knots of being, sit with me a moment, watch the white May clouds lose their fear of omniscience?

I've given up on Cold Mountain, given up on spring (almost) given up the chase after freedom from the mind's fragmentation bowing to the omnipotence of velocity's charms, nails bent in laughter, Buddha body I began making stopped at the bellyful of wood-fired chicken-sausage pizza w/ heirloom tomatoes, horseplay the closest I get to equanimous mind, or the poem moment, or lost in the presence of artful stone.

> Dogwood blossoms
> in Mr. Washington's backyard
> elevate the bloodline.

Ride the vehicle that's no vehicle there's no traffic jam just streams into memory's stretch. AH he'd say and she'd 2nd that & everything would still be empty except crow's belly fed on gutter crackers before we try to discern the meaning of this latest rain/remember rebalance the backyard stones knocked loose by one more errant & laughed-at hammer.

5:24P – 5.26.11
Seattle Subud House

27

25. Banknotes of Skin

Banknotes mellow and wrinkle as if they were made of human skin.

—Ramón Gomez de la Serna

Old as the skin of Northwind, his power – cold, his foe – Southwind, his astonished mouth yet another ovoid part negative space part fear of the power of Stormwind who could flick ancient trees & fling 'em in the river again & again & pile 'em up against the ice weir we walk above as we walk above the Monday Duwamish.

Billions of banknotes shrivel up in four more wars, must an empire get old & wrinkled before torn down & will the new boss write in characters & have the compassion of a Stormwind? Can we see the stones the icy weir became? Not at night. We learn to give proper proportion to foreheads, learn to accept the shudder as the physical manifestation of grace accept the last rays of the Seattle day's first bit of sun, make a pact with coyote within eyeshot of Yeomalt Point.

Learn to proper draw five warriors their eyes not exactly T's their six spears pointed & aimed, their gaze fixed for neverending battle their scholarship not limited to war.

An ovoid may be a void may be a circle may be an egg may be oblivious to the skin of dirty banknotes maybe an antidote to parlor tricks symptomatic of an evil empire's final doomed truth or may just be astonishment.

Leave Grandmother alone
with he who can lift century-old cedars
& remember memory lives
in all wrinkled skin.

8:44P – 6.5.11

26. Wind in the Stetsons

You can tell that wind can't read because when it riffles through pages, it always starts in the back.

—Ramón Gomez de la Serna

The wind can't wait to see how the poem winds up informs my Stetson straw hat before me of its arrival makes Jeremy's hair look like Donald Trump's, perfects a wave continues to be baffled by the Flower Ornament Scripture which tunes its birthless self to the celestial ear recommends Siddartha.

The wind forgot it was summer, fears the fierce bill of the hummingbird & its tracking skills, sends sounds of power saws drifting over Lake Xacuabš, dwelling in the diamond realm, fears not our age between gods.

The wind (when pictured) has a sad look on its face, always in a hurry not tracked by red light cameras, focused on liberating opiates from summer poppies aside the farmer's market dressed in drag.

The Seattle pre-summer wind's not here yet nor is Seattle summer, yet awaits the next CSA delivery, learns how to cook sunchokes, is stopped by the length of the pre-hairball cat neck, teaches without heedlessness, has attained ultimate wisdom & skillfulness, liberates sentient beings & greasy newspapers that've each served their final purpose before both of them either become, or act as, dirt. This wind's a field of blessings whipping pennants into froth. Much more gentle than Northwind (cousin to November & Stormwind.) Never seeks vengeance or recognition knows how that book winds up as a lust for one more, one more after that & only one more. The Dr. Pepper can signals something sexual in the dream. The celestial ear hears Mary as only one of many names the wind cries & the Tuesday morning dream face as omen of the power of much colder winds.

The wind's made of
sockeye skeletons in the sky
some w/ bellyful of eagle.

OFFICER of LAW
LIVES HERE

12:32P – 6.8.11

27. Wind & Insects

That fly which occasionally appears on your wrist is taking your pulse.
— Ramón Gomez de la Serna

& that dream of a wrist bone being a cist she sd Jon had removed's not cured by Odin's stave or the sound of wind pouring (confessing) its sorrows into a jar nor its stated intent to knock that dead bee off the reticent rhododendron in the spring of no spring nor is it the news they (the wind & its cousins) bring in waves like that summer night's lone freight train horn, no.

Not the dream neither of the next record getting on or Ralph Towner's *Jamaica Stopover* becoming the mantram for all this. A pick (plectrum) is what we made of strum as if the cat had one & strummed in an effort to rid itself of Pop's moniker *fleabag* or how a carved chip of bone might do. How we cd make the guitar sound as if three were playing but only one sans-pick Ralph Towner or one Michael Hedges still able to bring the funk out of *The Funky Avocado* (*off the chain* Bull'd say).

It's the west wind brings this news   this particular breath/mind as if the ancient photo (can photos be ancient?) that photo were her blowing the news in the wind from west of here around Montañas Olympicas below high clouds unimpeded by sun bounding all in its boundlessness. The plectrum strikes again & we are awash in harmonics & steam. Here the waterfall reinvents itself you can just click a button & it's all endless, each new wave of spray a healing shudder a prayer to the Bodhisattva of Compassion. She will not take you by the hand but leads anyway to one or all of thirty-three heavens, Jamaica only being a stopover, here's what we mean by transmission. Could be a bee, a piece of meat, an upturned bumbershoot or the last breath of the days light turning skyscrapers bright gold for a moment that you sometimes notice.

Ralph Towner flattens fingers & we're back in Jamaica again sending news to Cubans hungry for a new spice where culture has a chance to replicate. Frijoles negroes. The plátanos ripe enough for breakfast. Maybe you can make picadillo con chorizo de soy. The wind will always bring starlings but maybe today beneficial insects, another transmission   or   money.

Link between creator Gods & humans spirals up
& down. Wind   the original
world wide web.

8:43A – 6.9.11

28. The Cruel Majority (After Jerome Rothenberg)

He killed time in vengeful anticipation of what time was doing to him.

—Ramón Gomez de la Serna

& the empire to which he extends the profane six more wars: Iraq: *the dregs of counter-insurgency, militarized State Department, 5,100 mercenaries;* Afghanistan: USSR's Vietnam is now our ten years war; Pakistan: *Off-the-Books Drone War* with machines doing the work of men acting as jackals; Libya: *NATO & her cronies;* Yemen: another CIA *off-the-books* war & *The Global War of Terror,* presences in Somalia and 74 other states coerced to become part of the *cruel majority.*

The cruel majority afraid of the commons (born with a silver foot in his mouth) sneeringly say *socialism* and *save the fetus* but throw another baby in the fire. The cruel majority guards that fetus at gunpoint & assassinates the planned parenthood doctor. The cruel majority makes you work til you die, shits on the ground and says *mangia!* The cruel majority makes the planet conjure tornadoes on steroids, ignores the apocalypse, watches the Connecticut River get sucked into the sky & pulls the blinds on tighter.

The cruel majority gave you napalm & Abu Ghraib, A–Bombs & for-profit prisons, attaches electrodes to your testicles then jabs the pencil further in your ear. The cruel majority pulls out your right eye & jabs the burning stick in deeper. The cruel majority professes their faith with bumper stickers & Jesus fridge magnets.

No one stops the cruel majority except the cruel majority when it eats its own tail its own children eats Doritos eats off its own arm as the voices of the Donner party ring in its ears. The cruel majority listened to the wrong wolf favors anal electrocution for suspected terrorists calls it the *faggot flag* can't hear his own screaming God can't wait for this lifetime of hell to be over so invents new hells of pestilence & microwaves another cheese pizza.

All hail members of
the Cruel Majority, the enemy
we keep feeding.

3:35P – 6.15.11

29. Into the Eight Directions
(Octopus Mom)

Lizard: the brooch on the garden.

—Ramón Gomez de la Serna

& the jewels escape from a mother who will give birth, tend thousands of eggs, turn gray & die. Not unlike the nets of gems & honeysuckle appearing spontaneous in the backyard, under a buddha's feet & out the wombs of octopus mom ensconced in a den of concrete, bricks & rocks deep under surface of the Sound.

     Thousands of eggs laid, tended seven months latticed into egg chains & attached to the roof of a den off Alki. Eggs groomed in bubbles kept free from predators, bacteria & algae teardrop eggshape saffron-yellow gorged on yolk. Two maybe three live. The octopus den mom won't eat, blows oxygen-rich water against the eggs, blows them out of the den when time & grays til death.

     Under the Sound too's a garden, extends throughout ten directions with opals & jade bull kelp & otters phytoplankton & hermit crabs urchins & bloodstars. Proportionlessness tips of octopus suckers contain myriad universes extend into ten dimensions, turn gray & remember the gravity of emptiness after four short years.

    Octopus mother
   we feel your courage above all sounds
  pass on the calamari.

1:37P – 6.22.11

32

30. The Day the Weather Decided to Die
(After a Haida tale told by Robert Bringhurst)

On hearing the wooden rumble of thunder we realize that we are situated below the platform of the sky.

—Ramón Gomez de la Serna

What constitutes a good family they say and give instructions to servants under the backdrop of the hugest sucking sound in history prelude to when the wind'd no longer rumble from under the skirt of the great Ma   no longer float a blue heron's Xacho-side lumber no longer sustain.

Age of celebrity tattoo news   of the rise of Yurok Duwamish Tsimshian Haida Puyallup Muckleshoot Musqueam of tornadoes hurricanes earthquakes tsunamis bee silence Fukushima and Fukushimas to come.

The weather born out of cockleshell embryo   or   out of snot, weather that hunts birds and sends winds out in the skins of blue jay, weather that steals hats of campesinos (compassions) for kicks weather that would sprout houses when adopted by a master carver weather that would be a scholar of carving.

The weather when painted would sit facing the sea would weep for owls with spots and the new northward range of dolphin's neighborhood weather that would warn of the Big Ones who think of biting   weather whose big fish story is dried halibut & waits & waits & waits for a shift in settler rituals.

It could start with *today is a good day to die* could start with the inheritance of the campesino   (compression) who opened up about his daily prayers for humility or when he (the one born in a cockleshell) wd dress as wren & sit way above the sea as a cumulus cloud waiting to see what his latihan would bring: dance, song, chant or something more cathartic just beyond his   out stretched   wings.

Remember: crow's yr brother, stumps
never lie, WE
hold up the sky.

6:34P – 6.25.11

31. Dragonfly Resurrection

Horse flies are smudges on the air.

—Ramón Gomez de la Serna

Dragonflies are silent fireworks. Into the heart of a carnivore we go & see her arrive 30mph on the solstice see her *stalk the rushes & sedges   recon the ponds   work the grass tips*   maybe let the fresh sperm be scooped out to mate again maybe see you out thousands of individual eyes maybe shoot up to spy another dragonfly 125 feet above.

Dragonfly older than dinosaur cardinal meadowhawk filigree skimmers western forktail coal-fronted threadtail Apache dancer Aztec dancer   immortal   unreliable   more spark than flame more action than lengua mala more meat eater than lilac-sniffer more drunk than your last hallucination   four wing'd independent flight.

Gauzy wings glitter
in summer solstice
sun.

7:04P – 6.25.11

34

32. Bear Camp Road

The cedar is a well that has become a tree.

—Ramón Gomez de la Serna

& so living on borrowed teeth (& weaning) we head south to Celilo (Wyem) Falls Chief Tommy Thompson watching it fall under water & it's still there, radar says, submerged. The large ghost village still feeding gov't housing first people the shrine now in the hearts of shriners, south we go

over lava now atop cinder cones via red roads & see everything, Three Sisters, Mount Jefferson, Three Fingered Jack, Broken Top, Bachelor, calderas waiting to fire & we living on borrowed teeth await the ancestor avalanche to stunt every settler cancer.

South (still) & west to what was Mazama now a caldera they call a crater un azul beyond Miles, beyond Joni, beyond Patricia Barber bluer than July Cascadia sky bluer than the eyes of Almondina blue   a blue that floats Wizard Island, blue on which pine pollen floats in magnetic clouds & watches eagle flybys and expires blue.

South still & stumble upon Bear Camp Road. A road to the Rogue, a death road. James Kim floating for help in December Big Windy Creek leaving a wife and two daughters at the snow-bound Saab wagon or camper salesman Dewitt Farley not taking chances on his legs (or survival) but puts himself in the hands of his Lord his posthumous journal says, never again a view of the pacific blue beyond Gold Beach.   Bear Camp Road, the only route to the Oregon Coast north of California and south of the Rogue. *Narrow, rugged & crooked. Not suitable for travel in winter.* Bear Camp Road.

Carry water
pack a lunch
or two & update yr
dental records.

9:40A – 7.11.11

35

33. No Cigars For Potato

He selected it as if he were choosing a flute instead of a cigar.

—Ramón Gomez de la Serna

& kept talking & exhaling though the ancestors were exhorting the other
& kept getting burned running out of breath wondering why the fires were
why they were getting larger who with all this fuel *choking on his youth*
Cedar'd say   crying like an Ivan Osokin with another chance at Spanish
another chance for initiation a legacy & organic food, doses of your refined
voodoo & pins in the wall.

                    In the summer of no summer
it was a summer of sweeter Rainier cherries (those left by crows or Stellar
Jays) & rain. Road trip summer the GPS tracking lefts & rights to Stanley
Park's Lost Lagoon where Heron's still (waiting) on top of the diving
platform where ducks & geese nevermind the tourist circumnavigators.

Hecho en Cuba totalmente a mano like his mother, maybe a baby learns to put
the right accent on it to avoid potatoes & studies the science of fire & breath
& their dancestep in service of the hereditary liver & breath here, where I
fish around for a waking dream or its equivalent learn to savor July rays,
step away from the cigar keep, as big daddy says, keep the end out of sight
just a cessation in the series just a pause to live, smell the English Heather
& incubate a ring out of anything but a revolver.

              See what you see
                 says he
         hornets building their palace
     in July Cascadia rain.

9:02A – 7.18.11

34. War on Silence

If there is too much applause after a symphony, the audience risks rubbing out its memory.

—Ramón Gomez de la Serna

As Cage left 4:33 for you to fill & no one heard his prayer. In the mid-50s Miles told Red Garland to play like Ahmad Jamal. Space to separate notes. Now I have the technology to completely anaesthetize myself from the demands of the industry-generated culture on my t-mobile samsung smart phone.

Civilians want a no flight zone over Montañas Olympicas where one square inch   of silence begins to combat the *evil is mechanical,* combat the war against silence. Construction workers down the block say *no* as they pound their semi-delivered machines all morning starting at 8. Cops say no as their sireeeeeeeens wail all night's hours. Sword ferns en garde & will get the last thrust. Ferns & moss. Away from the Hoh River.

Monk would lay out, spin around, slow the earth's rotation, add gravity to Coltrane's solo. Left foot still, right foot slips away to realms unknown to we civilians. Pave a path of silence between angles for Charlie Rouse.

& the moment after another sacred Salish song the hand would find an orbit from the heart to the sky to the heart as an amen. As Thunderbird speaks. As an e haichka. An almost silent prayer.

Rain resumes.

10:33A – 7.25.11

35. Qinghai Sunflowers

Cats eat the rat of time.

—Ramón Gomez de la Serna

But the cat passes on the lychee nuts, can't scratch 'em open. Fascinated by Beijing dragonflies & triangular stacks of grain in Xining backyard gardens & sunflowers! Count the steps of the Qinghai sun much closer from 3K meters.

(Tui) ☱

Aware or not, we've arrived *In Search of the Absolutely Blind Encounter* & know the ghosts will be repelled by blackness, that it's the stripes of our own mind we must repel or re-direct into their most natural shape. Morning *Meat Package* & a bracket fungus awaits. The husk of the sunflower seed she spits flies into the Qinghai wind.

(K'un) ☷

Head to the gigantic salt lake, itself a sea to Tibetan people, a 4,500 click large teal mirror eats the sky. I have a prayer flag vision etched into my memory & rocks that will forever remain sacred. She has a Tibetan Cowgirl hat & a stuffed Tibetan Mastiff and a museum mask to scare the terror out of would-be evil-doers. Tourist photos riding well-groomed show yaks. Maybe a manifestation of the *God of the Lake* who would smile on a poetry wall, who would comfort Lorca from beyond his nameless grave & again thank Guo Muruo for helping spread the peace wave of one Walt Whitman, one with all.

> Learn to take a
> > toasted Qinghai watermelon seed
> split it with yr teeth.

9:04A – 8.16.11
Tongren, China

36. Taming Power of the Small

Tourism: The Art of Fleeing.

—Ramón Gomez de la Serna

& the lone mosquito who has severed herself from Xi Chuan's tiger or leopard or chimpanzee strikes again in the Beijing night snacking on the sweet blood of tourists just before the bureaucrat can take his hack before he too plunges into the *crevices of history.*

(The taming power of the small. The feminine force gains ground.) And so go to the Yellow River before it turns yellow, follow your Bön haunches to watch Monks learn html, let a cellphone call go through to voicemail, lug a case of pepsi to lunch of tsampa, pea gelatin (shan nyu), corn & toasted watermelon seeds but no green tea with lychee nuts. You may slap yourself in introspection or let the Chinese hotel foot masseuse do it with a wooden (wounded?) hammer. You hope the divination of the mosquito flying out of the suitcase is incorrect. You may petition the *Fierce Vajra Who Takes Control of Unclean Places* or hope for blue wolves dancing in a sea of flames but all you really need's the photo of *Four-Faced Guardian of Free Mind* in front of you on which you meditate
   & take on appropriatequalities of aura-expansion & wise menu choices.

Again I say:
             Thunderbolt or diamond.
             Which way will you look
       when the bell rings?

8:55A – 8.20.11
Xi'an, China

(Hsiao Ch'u)

37. Power of the Pocket Journal

Those tiny pocket diaries make the year smaller.

—Ramón Gomez de la Serna

& a year will fit in two pocket journals will fit 400 or so seventeen syllable sentences will take on myriad dream images. There will be dreams of penis heads restrained by Eddie Vedder's sutures. The will be a Big Hump Fire burning over a thousand Olympic acres & Coltrane's *My Favorite Things* not quite drowning out the sounds of a cat on the way to the shelter.

It's in the pocket journal those Qinghai memories of toasted watermelon seeds & tsampa lessons of sugared je yogurt & vivid detail of the thangka *Consort of Tantric Deity Who Responds According to Prayer.*

> (Your puny prayers
> add muscle in the
> age of great velocity.)

So, you date them add a *please return* hope the pages don't stick so you skip or frighten yrself with the notion of a day of no sentence. You chart your life by 'em far from the Nepali woman who stitched the latest one which carries pressed flowers from your day on the Great Wall, the day she said with amazement in her wet-the-booth Akasaka way: *We're walking on the Great Wall of China!*
You leave board mutinies to another bit of cloth & pixel where dreams of the odd dark meat have you chewing toughness again but being civil about it or a line overheard: *If I promise someone a blanket, I give it to them* & how Mary Summer Rain knows it's solace & you tell no one you know where the tracking device is because you don't bring your legal evidence to the futbol pitch you know when the wind blows you'll see a chicken's ass & a legitimate petition to that side of the veil makes this one sweeter w/ a local porter & view of a Big Hump Fire sending smoke signals to beckon September pilgrims.

10:22A – 9.12.11

38. The Barking of the Bitches

The barking of dogs bites us.

—Ramón Gomez de la Serna

Cut into what's left of summer, shit on the lawn, keep cats on alert but never notice them as cats are people who in Allen's parlance *notice what they notice*. The waves of barks recede but the dinner table pile remains. Cashews, tissues & a camping toothbrush. Sunglasses new business cards & a Cascadia Cheese Festival ad with map ripped out from The Stranger. Memos, Chinese quail stamps & the Selected Poems of Yi Sha, what the Chinese Muslims call Jesu Cristo.

& more.

Golf tees, wha guru chew & SPLAB correspondence. Prisoner letters for little people, filtered water (7 oz down, 73 to go) & a hearty cardigan, not needed now that summer's awakened for one more three day bender, out like lamb chops & Fall in like chalk dust on book piles. Not sure what irks more, dog barks or car tires in interviews. How it took 2 seasons to recognize the thimbleberry bush 20 feet to my left. How the cleansing comes amidst an avalanche of lies that remind me of my sneaky youth before setting eyes on the Whulge.

Cascadia repels
white mans wars
but can one recognize the shape
of allies?

Communal living, they say & the mind brought back to a Tibetan medicine show half a world (Rebkong) away when begin the nightly pill ritual to: "Calm the nerves, calm, passes after detachably, the well-distributed vitality, awakens the brain to straighten out…" that which a Raven might call *passive-aggressive, needy, ungrounded, and a little perverse in an odd way*. That which brings on a whoooooooosh of antepasados & a cleanse. That which separates the bitches from those loyal critters who'd rip out the burglar's throat in a New York moment.

Ah, Monday morning!

9:31A – 9.19.11

39. The Jewel Net of Indra's Shoe

Knives shudder when they have to cut a lemon.

—Ramón Gomez de la Serna

But the Soma therapist smiles & applies cocoa butter to his right elbow. Shudder & release. Tendons vet cement. There is a child in the basement locked in the position fetal & a fetus feted w/ nicotine & the notion no one here gets out alive.

There's a bubbling spring itching & skin & nerve as ally but who sees it that way in the land where cash makes you free (they say) & few mourn forest death. Montana mountainside evergreens eaten by beetles turn red (eaten by beetles). Colorado aspen die of thirst. Euphorbia trees in South Africa can't take the heat, find their own fetal position into which to curl. Northern Algeria Atlas cedars, down, down. We cremate Siberian forests, ignore the explosion of Australian Eucalyptus & the carbon every tree sucks in from our pizza delivery man while the smug Prius driver quietly glides by.

> Apricot sunset
> for one October moment
> makes gold poignance
> of the Beacon Hill sky.

Or a campfire escaped their gaze turned 1,100 acres into the Big Hump blaze turn my Olympics in the year of dam removal into sunset-marker. Turn my own blue flame into something like that which takes Pop, one Republican dirty trick at a time.

K1, the spring bubbles up from the bottom, salves palpitation, lets the Tibetan medicine man know a heart here breathes in each blast of carbon & exhales shoeshine for one more jewel in Indra's endless net.

7:43A – 10.2.11

42

40. Mobocracy 101

He touched the keys in his pocket to get home sooner.

—Ramón Gomez de la Serna

& then rescued Ramón from the garage. That is no place for a dead surrealist neo-barroco poet. Sure, it's no spider-infested Slaughter basement, but dusty full of cat hiding places the sounds of rain & neighbor chickens.

Put him in Tahrir Square. Put him in Zuccotti Park (but call it Liberty) or at Westlake Center a molotov cocktail throw from Niketown & the failed monorail. Put him with the 99% of us acting in class self-defense away from any of the 1,000 military bases the imperialists use to perpetuate the American nightmare of Mickey Mouse & Ronald McDonald hand in hand with Kim Phuc fleeing Dow Chemicals burning all but the sky. Put him next to Troy Davis & the electric chair (or table) on which the people of Georgia administer their lethal injections.
                                                Put   him   in
Afghanistan at the fatal wedding party or on the business end of American drones. So boneless are they who send bots to wage war (or mercenaries.) Put him in the boardroom of Xe or Blackwater or School of the Americas, anywhere they plot terror. Let him be their wall's fly though more like a beetle or spider, smiling, dropping hints about cats & their perpetual Sunday or their method of communication, one tail to the underside of the leg. One plutocracy fearing the wrath of the 99 & we are coming & we are hungry & we are running out of time.

            One big monkey wrench
        stockbrokers never pondered,
     w/ the familiar stench
                of democracy.

3:52P – 10.10.11

43

41. Othila's New Muscle

What the celebrity glimpses in his fame is a presage of his own death.

—Ramón Gomez de la Serna

What the Raven glimpses from his own feathers is that they're dyed. What the 1% gets from life will be dust sooner than the decay of sound waves from the sax solo on Sensei – waves echo in rocks, the tide, the fall of the autumn oak leaf liberated by crow's landing. We wait for the 5th world (word) will it be flood or burn? Will we've time to make bone prints on the sky's rooftop or, after the orange shafted flicker, search for acorns on wavetops?
                    Here's an evolution, being at home was Robin's point. *A thousand times more dainty frog meat taste filled than ten thousand postcard yaks* he says as if he'd be string in the ring in the yak's nose the Tibetan yanks w/ a right hand for a photo op. The narcotic of capitalism vs the narcotic of righteous anger in a march on chase bank formerly of Manhattan. Through this I seek the common thread to my consciousness.
                                        Picture the Falling Leaf Moon's wax eaten by Wolf himself he who turns light into fur no nappier than Coyote's, she who is reflected as a Star above an Owl above a Raven w/ a human face. As if we were still all people all people (most of the time). This common thread this Jacob's ladder this skin boat to the 5th world does not end in flood or heat or steam but in beams like the one illuminates cherry red October rose hips, rosa rugosa after the first frost, in Lucile sun. How would any self-respecting Roque not say AH to that?

               Grandmother
          take my Raven face, let my
                    skimpy prayers add muscle
          & shine.

6:41P – 10.14.11

42. Capitalismo
(After Michael McClure's Mad Sonnet for Allen Ginsberg)

The vapor from a newly opened bottle of champagne is like the smoke from a dueling pistol.

—Ramón Gomez de la Serna

On this cold gray Friday late morning I walk the concrete valley of Westlake – a park hastily designed to meet the needs of capitalists with little real green. I dream the man can't be known takes a chainsaw to the walls as the music is changing & the walls of the city?

THE WALLS OF THE CITY SHUDDER for what's to come, money-strength on the cold concrete awaits peak oil day, vines already begin their climb on electrical wires above the banks of Lake Xacuabš. My bet's on the Himalayan blackberry bush.

Bankers & corporate puppets only too happy to dance their tune/point bullets at how the other 99 might live well & remember, in the vast recesses of whatever imagination's left, the ouroboros moment, how the cancer of casino capitalism can only end in eating the young. Or our tail. The 99% are people, just like you. Just like soylent green.

> *The moving beauty of their own*
> *physical figures*
>   await
>   the chapter after
>   casino capitalismo.

10:47A – 10.15.11

43. Wheel (Whorl)

Her hands withered but her rings did not.

—Ramón Gomez de la Serna

Her eyes saw the spindle whorl in Fraser Canyon above Yale. His eyes saw the deity & his throat named it darshan. The eyes have it. Meat memory of looking out cats eyes, looking out Raven. Looking from behind a heavy wingbeat whoosh whoosh can only be Raven (or Eagle). Out the eyes of a Karl Rove what one misses (has forgotten) sin darshan. Out the eyes of a grandfather instead or out the eyes of a grandmother out the eyes of a Roque. Cards flip on the table lit by white candlelight.

There is honey here (miel) there is tobac. There are fotos here. There is a goddess. There is a non-dominant hand involved & a catch in the throat. The lad in the grassy field before the mountains has a tool. (Coins). Up Fraser Canyon from Yale more eyes, Snake, Bear, call it Deer, Coyote, Chapmans, Hell's Gate, Boston Bar, call it Sasquatch. The wheel spins again, the rings hang on as the skin draws back into Marmot, Pica, the eyes of Yellow Warbler, Gray Jay, Mountain Chickadee.

So tired of paying bills minimum credit card payment student loan two choices: 1) Occupy 2) Spin the wheel/ return through the eyes of the other, Nutcracker, Ground Squirrel, Mule Deer, call it Elk, Moose, Goat, call it Kingfisher.

Ignore the clearcuts, find
the eddy of eyes. From
the center, spin the wheel
again.

10:02A – 10.19.11

46

44. Stellar (Ella)

Ships sail so far away, even farther, that their smoke is no more than the distant signal of a marine volcano.

—Ramón Gomez de la Serna

& further still the cosmos. & in the cosmos the soul that would be Ella. (Stellar). She. Her. No podemos hacerlo sin Ella. (Ella) as a constellation, a construction out the womb of the wily Almondina. Ella as a further lesson in the sacred feminine for one too slow to grasp but not so hopeless to not get another her.

      The ship's an ultrasound on goop upon a womb. Here, a radar beep. Here the sex sticks out. (Gender.) We can both bawl now or ready placenta recipes. "In some cultures...

      Two cats couldn't cut it, so out to the stars. (Stellar overdrive.) Two hearts & a half beating the womblights out on that vanilla latté. The cloud is faint again, but it's a star cluster, the light farther away than the smoke of a distant ship (skin boat) & all the captain said was "engage." All we had was velocity & building up the part that won't rot. & letting go the rest so they may in turn remember their dust & we can turn our sights back to the inky wet of the Cascadia night sky.

      Ella, she is
             we're listening & seeing that
    flashing beat makes ours   beat harder.

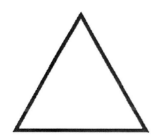
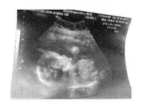

8:49P – 10.26.11

47

45. Cat Screams

Cats drink the moon's milk in the saucers of the tiles.

— Ramón Gomez de la Serna

Petition a Sibyl, wait for the space in the veil to crack open wider, shit in a box if yr lucky. Decline water for tuna juice. Become a familiar which elicits sobs when mind fotos of a corpse under a stoop are conjured. Chase the blue winged spiders out the hollow baseball dream moment & say they taste like crab.

Cats see the waves produced by *the twin of my vision* unbound, immeasurable & as much a person as chase or banco de America. Cats rub interminably itchy chin bones against file cabinets waste baskets any kitchen corner & go outside to die in a blizzard of oak leaves liberated by the first real noviembre viento.

Cat's meow for your oatmeal but won't eat it if you offer, want to lick what's left on yr plate after dinner tacos w/ sour cream & medium cheddar, know the auspicious time to walk away & die letting *"the dirt recede before my prophetical screams."*

Screams now only
as sobs grown gigantic.
Music a cat can hear.

7:32A – N.3.11

46. Wolf Ride

You don't hear death because once it is at home it goes around in slippers.

—Ramón Gomez de la Serna

Or on the pads of an Oregon wolf named OR-7 out the Imnaha Mountains cross 84 past Baker & Burns, lopes through deserts, ends up (for now) in forest, East Douglas County. Fear of reaper in slippers behind him the first here in 65 years 280 miles from home or so says GPS.

Only Algiz to protect linked by golden thread (or etherphone) to Asgard where all the good vikings (& their pets) end up. Past Hell's Canyon (wildlife highway) first of 1,450 now that the memory of the last wolf assassination fades (was back in '46) & the Wapiti unaware & the mitochondrial DNA evolves into a velvet medicine – tasty lunch for OR-7.

Here he holds on to the scent of hamingja – a spiritual force & OR-7, just wants lunch, maybe some tail, OR-7 8,717 feet in the sky atop Mt. Thielsen, Algiz somewhere hovers, view of Diamonds & mercy & this one wolf, tongue out to take the air's temp ready to help the Wapiti test how fast a pack of meat w/ antlers & four stomachs can run.

The quill of the day
rescued from the wolf of the night –
Odin laughs/rides OR-7

to parts south, two tongues hanging out.

10:41A – N.9.11

47. Occupy, Farewell, Spit

The moths which come out at night and fly at the window turn it into an aquarium of moths.

—Ramón Gomez de la Serna

Would turn again (re-turn) to flame, a torch, Kano *in my native tongue* again and see it *burn brightest where noble folk rest,* bask in acceptance, turn the wine bottle of wrath into something akin to fellowship. Kano Ken next of Kin, six in & beams of light shot from a solar plexus.

> *[fragment structures – serial poems –*
> *all having to do with materiality of*
> *form – having to do with death]*   *)*. Blaser

& the randonee of the plot resumes. Death. How Kano could point a blind eye toward it (in hopes of turning) w/ a torch. (What's entropic & what's the random shudder of the divine at play; where's the song, surely a Full Snow Moon moan will repeal the pull of recent nafsu.)

How we hunger for priest as king or something huger. How we'll occupy & occupy as a last grasp that which the bankers always ready to snatch, how 60 whales gave up, beached themselves to tourists, let go in New Zealand how the torch of Kano led them to finish at Farewell Spit. How to negotiate the ladder of life forces from the animal to human and to the divine without falling for (resorting to) a sand nap?

> *Your path is poetry* Robin sings from his own
> nap of dirt
> *your goal is beyond poetry.*

> Songs are what we are
> & will return to
> after this lucid dream
> we burn through.

10:41A – N.16.11

48. Torquemada's Revenge

Water has no memory: that is why it is so clean.

—Ramón Gomez de la Serna

Or maybe it's in latihan kedjiwaan twentyfourseven surrenders nafsu it attracts to wind, dirt or rock,   winds its way as a Fraser River through a North Arm or a Canoe Pass from above might be seen as November brown of salmon advancing gull or goose fighting the tide or in the teal of April's juveniles for when heron flexes dinosaur wings how can the wide eyed ones do anything but wonder?

& so goes it in an age where wonder meets truncheons (*billy clubs in my day* Bob'd say, nursing his own ribs bruised at an Occupy gone awry.) Wonder meets truncheons & Vaders & gas masks & a savant in the sixties said: "There is a time … when the operation of the machine becomes so odious, makes you so sick at heart, that you can't take part. You can't even passively take part."

What can one do to undo what the machine's done? How take apart the mechanistic or better grow huger (overcome) become human? Did Fa'Tsang ever see Fousang, the mulberry (or Hawthorne) tree 10,000 clicks east of his crib? Newton! His sleep crusts our eyes the creep of machines advances only so far as bodies in occupation let it.

> Watch the water
> (she'd say)
> for clues on surrender
> or torque.

8:40A – N.20.11

49. 49th Parallel Blues (After Nate Mackey)

The function of waves is to bring the salvage from shipwrecks.

—Ramón Gomez de la Serna

Went back to the book, had to flesh out what 49 was. Was a parallel, was a universe. A series of them. A quag was where they were headed, a world without soul or where soul was weak or with held w/ religious zeal. Back to the book for a whiff of an old song sung new, a star-eyed babe made real again out of meat & memory. Star dust & comet stuff. A tail raised at the end of an age end of yet another yuga.

A brother lost, perhaps for a time, yet another brother made up of mud, not as mad, almost as innocent. A bother made up of blood's memory a memento mori of sorts & still seeking sentience often lost between legs (or ahead of them), lost in the reeds as if the product of a bad shank or grief's weight abandoned finally shook loose how torque lost its pull, latter day Torquemadas lost their power, laughter cast its healing glance upon the mercenaries & left mercy.

Mercy's mission mumbled in the round, widdershins. Mercy's mumble infinite (or so it seemed) redolent, or so we saw, radiant or so the jewels in the net of Indra surmised. If it was quag to which we were headed we'd brake, we'd wrestle a wrench away from the monkeys or from the late capitalist hammer squadron. We could smell the quag coming & wanted none, wd find the wealth of wet cement to lay our head on, wd listen for dreams just this side of bricks & cayenne weapons way away from any gumbo. Where there'd be quag we'd beckon mercy w/ songs mumbled at first, right up past the gut's obstruction then bellowed into latihan air like a bapak wd, blown like Birks fat cheeks a monk's last remission a bird song hurled at the oncoming winds.

He'd sing it three times
& each time the word
mercy caught a wave, wd
begin to stick.

9:11A – N.29.11
over Montana

50. Nevermind Gray Waves

Frogs are always taking part in swimming races.

—Ramón Gomez de la Serna

Glass they say & Monet here would have a heyday. Mist not yet settled, instead a pink & ruffled part gray sky sun setting itself over Lake Xacuabš' Andrews Bay. Garry Oak so gold against coniferous you see it from the plane landing at SeaTac or circling to touch down.

How the weak ripples like violent still lifes Vincent made serve to reanimate reflections clouds leave somewhere above swimming frogs & turtles – herons not around & the treeline more visible before the first star emerges.

Who cd paint this scene every other day for two months as light fades, changes, brightens, catches stitches of Eritrean, Mandarin, español & echoes of Whulshootseed in waves beneath our feet. (Or bike tires.) The first lights from lakeside houses morse code a sign to the day's dying light –

Nevermind the gray
passes for rain.
I'll die here.

4:33P – 12.1.11
Seward Park

51. Echo in Licton Springs

The echo could take our place if it had a hat.

—Ramón Gomez de la Serna

Could find itself echoing off the wall at Licton (Liq'tid) Springs past David Denny's summer cabin site and the iron spring water bubbled up through dark red clay before Metro thought it ought run into the sewer.

Where Duwamish before would cleanse & grow cranberries where the Four Corners of Susan Point's galaxy mend their weave in red veins heading past mouths again in O. Red clay mouths, ovoid eyes & O's take us back an ice age or two. O's a possible option for the swallow adorning one's forehead forages for dream imagery.

Might be an echo of a cranberry or two in that noggin, might be a golf ball's echo rescued from a bad design or a car on your right shoulder you must carry until finding a parking place for it near the market where cranberries get lugged in from Grayland.

Honor thy river people awaiting the resilient echo of Alder, Maple & Chokecherry blossoms. The River God in love with his dreams & the stream that cuts wrinkles into his jay-beaten brow. The black Lab whose hair mighta made a mighty fine blanket whose lunge legendary upon the Stuck River to get a speeding stick going faster than Assman's miller can. The dog's echo   a bear in a dream – they gave him the name Japanese, Kuma.

River people (& their echoes)
at home in red clay
or in the silver river which only comes out
@ night.

5:55P – 12.4.11

52. Daughter of One of Seven Sisters

Those who choose to sit near the pedestal of monuments are taking a transfusion of immortality.

—Ramón Gomez de la Serna

& those who choose to navigate the cosmos feet first through the photon band offer a hand out to humanity. Those who choose to be conceived in a stew of Monkstone Theocracy seek a new angle in to what we humans are scheming to needle into these torturous days. I'd see a rung in the cosmic distance ladder a challenge any Jacob worth his matzoh would relish. I'd try a Puer diet always aware of the brilliant corners through which one'd pass on the way through a photon band. Alcyone high in the night sky could be a sly reinterpretation of Lady Day.

This Atlas holds many worlds on her wide shoulders & with 'em the outcome of woman vs machine. This Electra, no bird brain, queen of ravens whose big beak pecks a way through nebulae. This Maia too, dove-like & a scatted love song away from her own Mercury & sisters beyond, street lights above a silver ribbon, mileposts in a trek through galacticity. I Mean You was what I meant in the moment in which lightning bolts were grunted out ecstatic. Ella My Dear he may have wanted to sing had the notes any words that went with them though they sounded like oooooooo's and ayyyyyyyyyyyy's when chanted that way; when rebounded off the walls of the Latihan hall. Maybe a heyyyyyyyy there & nebulosity tracked 135 parsecs from our Sqbecsed-side situation.

Kick your way here, dear, we've a Monk tune or two for you. Kick your way here, Roque, the platanos are ripening. Kick your way here, daughter, we're scaling the path from animal to divine. Kick on girl

we're preparing for the view
from the hot blue
luminosity, for which
we've been angling

9:45A – 12.19.11

53. Nothing Death

A kiss is nothing in brackets.

—Ramón Gomez de la Serna

A poem's nothing on paper. A steller jay's a punk in a western vista. Any death's an opportunity. One wd sing his pop a harmonium-laden blues w/ gurus & aunties in the same field as genius & uncles wondering what pain'd come at the end, maybe ass cancer. Who wants to write an elegy? Who's aware of the avalanche the ancestors plot?   Who wants that tower card to appear in the reading on mortality?

The Chinese poet wd call it *complicated* & reach for the buddha roll, symmetry & mold on his jacket, 80 days of rain on his mind. The flight of the mosquito never far, fleas piss the dream clothes as the protagonist chews on pocket cedar.

A goodbye may be more enormous than you know, another nothing, this time between cups of pu'erh, down at the side of the winter river, keen in its protective fog, its own awareness of grief's velocity & riverduty to bring it all downstream where everyone lives, a grief field flipped to something more pliable.

Death's surrender between
Facebook meal photos. Here intellect cringes/
wishes
for something huger.

11:06A – 1.10.12

54. Black Dragon Year

The heart measures in blood everything that happens.

—Ramón Gomez de la Serna

The dragon stays stuck to lampposts at the boundaries, but *looks like a mountain lizard.* The ancient poet stays in the ear, but the ink he pisses is invisible. Emptiness stays in the river drunk on wheat & reflects back what we thought was dumped in the thick of a December Wednesday. The Black Water Dragon sits in the Black Walnut tree but the last leaf hangs on as if w/ fangs. The old poet sings of the world *that lies beyond the human* but gets no taste 'til death. The heart stays in the chest but appears at night as a constellation orchestrating movement of silver-colored blood that gains velocity in water years.

The politician stays in the middle & the middle moves so far right can't see its shadow can't tell the poem from rhetoric can't feel blood when it gets past the hat can't pass the hat to campesinos & amnesia gallops in to start it all again in animal rhythm impervious to grief.

Scorn stays west of the left ventricle the poet says & sees it stuck there unable to mutter anything but a GRAHHR or a muuurrrrfffffffff so writes a poem that becomes a series of poems that becomes a house & a whole slum of them headed for the same plight (evening) stuck in the shithole of his imagination   up near the top of the monkey puzzle tree to wile away the January afternoon hoping not to become lunch for Sasquatch/lost in the dust of a library archive waiting to return in another incarnation   or   vivid   hallucination.

The Black Dragon
waiting for the poem to end
burns the bacon to a crisp.

12:03P – 1.12.12
After Xi Chuan's *Somebody* and
Li Bo *Questions Answered*

55. Fear is Salty

The important thing is to be happy, even while typing.
—Ramón Gomez de la Serna

Even in a dragon year, a water dragon year, the dragon at the core
of literature's carved as a country might, or a pig, a goat, or large
intestine like Pullman, Washington. Pop pulled grief out of that hat as
if it were his teenage brothers with the worst sore throats ever, gray
film coating them, hoarseness & abnormal cardiac rhythms & don't get
me started on skin.

Or the ancestor warmed in my blood awakes after a
thousand years, no longer waiting for god, no longer happily stuck in
the phalanges ready to remember the last photograph of Pop smiling
ready to rescue the memorial balloons stuck in his family tree.

Fear is salty,
at least that's what old Chinese say & how it enters the bones from the
ears then to the bladder in winter one Seattle snowmageddon newscast at
a time, beyond where fences get erected on mountains to keep rocks from
playing in the road but close to winter & kidneys & ancestors.

Even in a
dragon year, a water dragon year, the dragon at the core of literature is
carved up like a country, or pig, goat, or large intestine, one can only
watch, wait, hear the January wind whip through firs and cedars or
watch ripples of the maple tree reflection in your afternoon teacup
totally unconcerned about style, or dragons, or the slow tortured death
of capitalism one bankruptcy at a time.

Just about to the labrynth's
center, far be it from me to remind you
you're almost halfway there.

8:04PM – 1.20.12
Whiteley Center
San Juan Island

56. Shooting Starward

The most terrible thing about our address book is that they will use it, inevitably, as the means of communicating our death to friends and relatives.

—Ramón Gomez de la Serna

& up past the San Juan spot where Death Camas sleeps in chthonic ecstasy & Fawn Lillies, Lupine, Chocolate Lillies, Indian Paintbrush and, yes, Shooting Star ready their April avalanche to right the sadness of the old man who can't empty himself to be a vessel for a throaty hymn to old age.

First - a small rosette of leaves one flower stalk shoots starward, branches to multiple buds that nod down. Then purple-magenta blossoms unfold petals arch back aim starward. (Shooting Star.)
                    The old poet said *Sex is the mysticism of materialism* & how can one not love the lichenclimb up ghost limbs of the fir   how can one not love the kiss Sunday wind gives it further up how not see the sun radiate over the January Salish sea & not see a bit of themselves released skyward hoping for a soft landing in the sand of Grandmother's Cove?

                    Reductionism wd wonder (at best) or laugh at how *1/62,000th of the original mother essence, undetectable in any chemical analysis* & here we're halfway to the center of the labyrinth dreaming how to pet the Water Dragon in its holy holy moment   how trust that *chance will intervene and save the day*   how the rain when turned on its side hits the face like a needle   how the flicker found her way here, Salish seaside, only to disappear in a blur of red.

                 Sacrifice an Irish pig
              at the feet of two armies
            see who's man enough to shoot

        starward.

                              11:09AM – 1.22.12
                              Whiteley Center #7,
                              San Juan Island

57. Frog Song

The poet looked so long at the sky that he grew a cloud in one eye.
                                    —Ramón Gomez de la Serna

There was nowhere left. Each way the spindle'd whorl, no where there. No sea sky lake tree leaf grass stem left. They'd settle for a ghetto island settle for a frog place to put their skin on & cry. Cry for a mate. Cry to ward off a close encounter w/ some jealous ghetto frog. Cry just to get some.

By Imbolc or Candlemas we'd all be waiting for wood frogs we'd call the chorus we'd hear the silence as the 150'd rumble by & how they'd all creak up again once it was halfway past Slaughter. The day'd begin w/ woodfrogs end w/ woodfrogs under a woodfrog moon w/ a woodfrog word 'Kreek-eeck' it was (an ad) 'Kreek-eeck' it'd go way past the fred meyer the driver's ed lessons St. Vinny de Paul & the bike shop. 'Kreek-eeck' it went on   a whole night of frog fucking 'Kreek-eeck' he's on her back 'Kreek-eeck' neighbors get no sleep "Kreek-eeck' can you *fuckers knock it off already* 'Kreek-eeck' they'd try & fuck any silent thing that wander'd close. (Sober.) Then hitchhike to Alaska in a Christmas tree.

                                    Susan spins the whorl agin
& there is no sound here   there is no where there & less here & the frog whorl may have one for every direction, but her frogs are made of wood & her frogs are fetching but no substitute & 'Kreek-eeck's' when the wood needs some grease & 'Kreek-eeck' rarely the sound of some suburb. What's a ghetto anyway?

                Our canary
                        who's coal mine & when's
        winter end?

                                        3:41 – 1.23.12
                                    Whiteley Center #7
                                    San Juan Island

60

58. Coyote Guts

The eyes of the dead look at clouds that will never return.

—Ramón Gomez de la Serna

It was the First World. People'd not come out yet. People'd take a fur or skin, put it on take it off just like a coat or hat. Mosquito Flea Spider Ant big as cougars. Eagle Beaver Fox Coyote fish't & hunted dug roots lived in longhouses had sweat lodges & slaves   had chiefs & laws & were just, yes, the people. Fur people medicine people plant people   people the day before people beyond. People who'd shake when they needed a good hit of divinity who'd spit as a spit of antipathy who'd growl a grahhr when needed to ward off evil.

Coyote created the world or the world created Coyote or Raven created the world or the world created was created by the Man-Who-Changed-Things, some Changer he was & might of been Coyote still.

But the Old-One made the earth out of a woman. Soil as flesh rocks as bones wind/breath, hair of trees & grass & when she moves we tremble. & Old-One'd take strips of flesh to roll up the ancients as a potter might pinch off some clay, ball it up. & were Deer, Elk, Antelope people or half-people & were people meat? Pinch a bit of skin from earth add wind & these ancient ones

these ancient ones were dumb. Not couldn't talk dumb. They cd talk. Needed a guide, dumb. Needed a tutor dumb. & who'd they get to lead them into the promise who'd they get to kill all their ignorance who to kill the monsters, whittle the longest arrow who? The guy who dropped anvils from the cliff who. The one w/ the inside to all that is Acme the one who'd always crashland in a dustcloud the one'd bury all but his dickhead in dirt & trick the girls for kicks faking it was a ripe strawberry.

Power in the bullrushes.
Coyote gets the shortest arrow
& supernatural power
in   his   guts.

10:03P – 1.25.12
The Whiteley Center #7, San Juan Island

59. Sisuitl (Si'sEyul)

Every professor looking at the sea becomes a professor of Geography.

—Ramón Gomez de la Serna

Sisuitl (Si'sEyul) rode in on the back of an Orca or on the soul of an Orca a commandeer anyway one head for either direction. Ready your holly (or blood to spit) find his slime trail in which to step or petition a Thunderbird as this is not just another two-headed worm. It's a warrior god invincible, a magic chthonic war canoe navigating below ground rivers, guardian of the people whose house is in the sky.

Whose house is in the sky 'cept chulos del cielo 'cept a latihan that had gotten large 'cept any creature with Horn Power & the gift of flight or shifting shape for what the occasion calls. Whose house in the sky 'cept Sisuitl (Si'sEyul) who'd ride in on the back of Orca (or on the soul of one) in the guise of a worm who could get huge enough to block Commencement, huge enough to be human, self-propelled underground canoe, or make you stone for just one look. Whose house is the sky house darkening Cascadia one November storm at a time bobbing madrones/make pines sing?

> Dance with boughs
> of Western Hemlock, hand
> of holly, mouth
>   full of self-defense blood
>   to spit.

12:57P – 2.20.12
Lucile

62

60. Hymn to Indian Plum

The interlocking hearts carved on benches are the cheap wedding vows of seducers.

—Ramón Gomez de la Serna

& the book as spiritual instrument will not itself thicken your knowledge (will knot itself) will not itself allow yr vision to penetrate the evergreen nor the cliff above Obstruction will not itself lift you up out of animal blinders or make luminous the February witch hazel's view or the perched Anna's Hummingbird or the frail first candleflames of the Indian Plum, no.

Might make a fine window (widow?) to jump in & see the Light of the Supreme Lamp of Universal Virtue or Lion Banner of Universal Light, might be an in to the Subtle Light of Flames of Universal Jewels or the Banner of Oceans of Qualities of Universal Sounds. Cd open my February window and hear waves below bushtit chatter or starling gossip & jet engine wash. Maybe wait for a day when (through practice practice practice) could envision hearing the Pleasing Voice of Universal Awareness or the Undefiled Treasury of Light of Oceans of Cloudlike Sounds.

Could make
a topknot of that. Cd imagine it instead of a whorl of pheromones or a goatskin jailcell in which to feel the beatdown of bruxism. Could envision a Light   Banner   of Fragrant   Flames   each morning, before yoga & truckgrowl before slaughter and dehydration before the animal inside aware of extensive root systems   &   their   eloquent oceans of concentrations that sometimes emit the scent of magnolia blossoms or jalapeño or   jasmine.

Pick a vow
at least as radiant
as the first leafshoots
of the February
Indian Plum.

2:32P – 2.23.12
Lucile

63

61. Meat Again

Nothing forget us more quickly than a barstool.

—Ramón Gomez de la Serna

the sheer terror of being forced into incarnation in accordance with one's will one's agreement with the single intelligence. We watch at night after so much crying crying crying, cats as bed sentries naps as necessity (she who "could not nap" before finds it easy when exhausted). Crying crying crying how does a c-section inhibit the woman's body when will the milk come in when will the poems resume is she alive? I stroke a long thin baby finger to get a confirmation twinge.

The sheer terror of "this again" meat & all its needs, spirit forced back into the meat cage, mind forced back into a baby brain to chain the long slog back to embodiment of the interdependent origination she knows all too well now, but cries cries cries for an ounce of formula. Will it be pizza in 15 years? Corned beef hash? Narcotics, slot machines (not my daughter) stimulation who knows the social networks of the future maybe programmed surgically into nerves. Cappuccino? New hybrid foods (*fusion* they say) kim chi pierogies or something more simple?

The sheer terror of the replunge into meat again (*that's a lot of hair for a white girl*) & re-learning diaper technology after 20 years, car-seat & stroller tech (it's all in the gear) 60 days away from freedom she appears, a St. Patty's Day baby, parades every year on her day and Guinness like I had an hour after she arrived. Terror's antidote or hearty companion. She arrives.

> Meat again
> this scatter's namesake.
> The Runes say
> "reunion."

10:14A – 3.22.12

64

62. Buddha Bodies & Fake Train Horns

Even the thief of a mere fan was decapitated in China so quickly, and with such a sharp blade, that many corpses were never able to give a dying breath.

—Ramón Gomez de la Serna

Until September. September is a light w/ a Chinese tilt aimed at 22 whose white magnetic wind stretches out, vowels sung by cedars angled toward Venus. One's a muddle unadjusted to sunlight (or the Buddha body that beckons) while nine's love life lingers on lusting after threes (infatuated by salt) enacting age old water ceremonies – partial to dirges
& crow murders.

6, if preceded by nine's a cleansing ionic wave, wise as the uncle who grew up on Miles & shakuhachi solos. One still adjusting fascinated by shining objects especially golden or if scented by eucalyptus. (Madrones, but not much scent.)
April wants to be fearless as magnolia but lashes out – a boy whose pop left him in Queens to fight amongst Puerto Ricans, green but remembers past lives of pink turning white right in front of the fire. The fire that tempts seven, he w/ the wrath of Mars & blood-deprived cousins, he of arson & third world famines. Of soup lines & a fist full of failed derivatives getting some on the side of eight. Curling into an umber pocket or cave, waiting for clouds to lift or the turquoise morning to appear.

A blossom or two
shy of the Late Train Horn Moon.
(Fake it when the baby ain't
crying.)

11:37P – 5.2.12

63. Her Birthday, My Velocity

The Creator keeps the keys to all navels.

—Ramón Gomez de la Serna

(See picture 2, the her first photo ever, May 17, 1991, 6P on the dot.) Right leg so straight, she's not happy & all that hair! The original hairy white girl. Anonymous nurse hands rubber gloved sucking out sputz & the 1st baby burrito blanket. I got a five yr truce w/ her arrival & reborn somehow in a more human image. Five days later Zappa-fied Daddy-hood – & it IS an M's fro yo cup on RR's head & sly grin at 1818 10th W. in photo 1.

By month 11 she was on her rocker, hair still growing, hands gripping, smiling smiling smiling. Smiling again the obligatory half-naked child picture this on the toilet, this time (she points out in ten year old calligraphy) w/ Jerry the stuffed teddy she got from Aunt Barb in her Dalmatian outfit gramma made, the child caption in shot 6 – she the happy kid. She the 102nd Dalmatian.

N.U.'s size awing the 7th grader fighting weight in front the Medill sign, but she'd overcome both. The longest hair ever at Aesculapia in Wilderville where Asshole Graywolf tried his venom on this sweet little kid, the first shot in my escape from him. She catalyzing again.

How Grandma looks so young on Orcas, Doe Bay, Otter Cove. That purplish tie & no gray beard with Janice & RR the fashion plate in California, 2 & 1/2 yrs old at Naomi & Henry's before their house would come up in my dreams as the Northridge earthquake about to hit & the house to be condemned, then canyon'd. This is too much.

> She'll get her chocolate
> & now her Stella.
> If I cd only reconcile life's
> velocity.

9A – 5.17.12

64. Sin Malicia

Living in one century would be like living in them all if one only knew how to look at stones with serenity.

—Ramón Gomez de la Serna

To slow velocity & clear the wisdom eye some other sort of sandman had a hand in sanding (de-greasing) the path into the cosmos' matrix, obscuring the birdsong so obviously awaits May Tuesday focus   as   if   the dead around here were no more than an acid eats away the possible. As if the water (when glass) a sign wind was blowing out or the stones were not grandfathers waiting centuries to bestow something will clear away grains of that wisdom eye-sand a large latihan cd not fix.

Here in the heart of the place may be Cascadia is an island – meaning body of land surrounded by water – meaning surrounded by sea – meaning vast metaphor for concentration   (sin fronteras) as Garcia knew – meaning the stones, each have some kind of marking on them are gates of sorts, are to be selected for their pleasing color then situated on an altar-to-be-named later for the resonance, the hold, the stories they may evoke, the uncertain serenity of living in all the centuries at once in the millennium of instant karma, or velocity.

There were as many of them as atoms in a Buddha world & were all Thunderbolt-bearing spirits as if clouds had sounds dwelling wherever a Buddha was going wherever necessary w/ only the weapon of their guile which protected, clarified & never strayed from the direction festooned by the new light green shoots of the May Tuesday evergreen, metaphor for the heart's ripening family ghosts're determined to evoke.

Here stones
may've had enough to eat
don't need to feast
on the future.

10:22A – 5.21.12
Mala, Doe Bay,
Orcas Island

67

65. Dirty Raven Light Thief

The fountain of the contented garden sprays sky instead of water.

—Ramón Gomez de la Serna

& while we were Adam & Eveing our creation, in Haida Gwai they (& other cosmologists indigenous) figured a better agent. One'd be "deceitful, insolent, libidinous and often grotesque..." with a "penchant for scatology." Never mind he'd be a rock star in the darkness of USAmerica's 3rd century. A décepteur.

Before the Great Flood came & receded before starlings cd be seeded in Parque Central Nueva York, before trees could crawl up here from parts south before salmon found a nice nest in every Cascadia river before the J-Pod scooped up Ilalqo copepods & crustaceans & waaaaaaaaaaaaay before Sophie Charlotte von Mecklenburg-Strelitz. Darkness was not a metaphor not an adjective it was a condition – sin sol – it was the inky Northwet night sky all day all night not even a star or a Moon of Pure Awareness, no Wolf Moon, no Ripe Plum Moon, nada hermano.

But an old man on the bank of a river in a house with one daughter & no wife & his daughter cd be ugly as a slug but loved anyway. In a box in a box in a box in another box & another & another & a few more in the total dark there was light. & Raven eavesdropping heard about it & Raven desirous wd have to have it. & Raven studied the old man & daughter's riverside house but cd not find the door or even a window, but studied the daughter's walk & cd recognize her footsteps & when she went to fetch water he turned himself with his magic décepteur powers into a hemlock needle in her handful of water to drink, was swallowed, & grew inside her & was born a long-beaked, occasionally-feathered freak of a boy with shining eyes & a cry that split the night, curled hair & imagine his terrible twos. & Raven, he used that cry to get just one box, how cd Grandpa say no? & just one more & – well you know how it's gonna end. Caught in his jaws the light inside the last box, he, back to old Raven & wingbeat symphony out the smokehole to transform the world, stunning: the views of mountains against sky, ineffable: the shine of the silver river from the azul above, awe of water falling off the side of a mountain catching light beams in its decent & no more flying while blind. If not for Eagle, he'd a hung on to that light, but half of it slipped & broke off into one large piece & shards innumerable (became Moon & Stars) & Eagle kept pursuit beyond the rim of the known world, out East.

Back at rio rancho, Grandpa was sick about the lost light, sat above a growing puddle of snot & tears. But the dropped light entered the house & for the first time ever Grandpa could see his daughter was not an ugly slug, but revealed to be as beautiful as the first light green shoots of the May evergreen bobbing in late afternoon sun, beautiful as the ocean's shimmer when the mid-day sun hit it just the right neon'd angle, a little piece of him who'd tell his stories when he went back to meet his maker & wd laugh or cry thinking of the bedtime songs he'd sing to her to let her know everything was going to be ok. & it was, even after that dirty Raven did what all dirty Ravens always do.

If you're gonna keep yr light
        in a box
        at least keep yr mouth shut.

7:17P – 5.23.12
Mala, Doe Bay,
Orcas Island

66. Doors of Liberation

It is the slowness of its progress that assures the tortoise of longevity.

—Ramón Gomez de la Serna

Watching tortoise can be a door of liberation or sunset, south & east when setting Cascadia sun scatters pastels, a door of liberation in the instant setting up *oceans of inconceivable adornments* this moment itself a jewel Wilson Duff knew as an episode related to all past episodes & prehending ones yet to come, all doors of liberation of *all-sided observation of the universe.*

Duck couples hunt seaweed in the low-tide cove where Kingfishers wait in trees doors the same as much as the vaportrail left by Hummingbird after sugar rush at the downtown whale station doors of liberation much as the albino deer munching Pink Ladies sliced & thrown to the forest floor just this side of the garden fence cutting off all doubts, clarifies path to compassion for those you'd want to choke the shit outta, or whose land you'd like to treat like a grab bag but somewhere conscious these are episodes passing, jewels in mid-afternoon Thursday shimmer only the latest in the endless archetypal parade of doors of you know.

> Your cellphone not as likely
> to save you   as Eagle
> chased Raven 'til he dropped the
> last box of light.

9:51P – 5.24.12
Mala, Doe Bay,
Orcas Island

67. The Harmless Eccentric

The violinist holds his ear to his instrument as though overhearing a telephone conversation.

—Ramón Gomez de la Serna

Spirits come in and they go out syllables, at least that's what Jack believed & Robin & others who might've had a hand in the sky for the episode we could call latihan. But Jack had too much nevermind w/ single malt & the best become dirrrrrty shitttters too late to needle the Sea of Blood.

The martyr'd field only grows more luminous trying to embrace the Snow Moon's reflection in motion so slow, no one notices. Tired legs carry the fired-by-Indians burden no burden but episode no mere episode yet past love's answered moan where a baby waits in Blake's post-Newtonian universe underneath the obsolete constellations.

Dogen says: "when you find your place where you are, practice occurs" & de Chardin: "action has no value other than the intention which directs it." The people here first knew that from here to Yakutat & tried to tell us but life was not attuned to the movement of stars forgoing the promised gifts of the possible storm for the forlorn American art of entrapment. In the end the sea will shimmer, the green of the swallow's back reflect sun

the largest beard? The harmless
eccentric   who keeps time
aboriginal.

1:43P – 5.25.12
Mala, Doe Bay,
Orcas Island

68. Sowilo-Tinted Vision Field

When motion pictures were invented, the clouds in photographs began to move.

—Ramón Gomez de la Serna

Many (neglected) relocated to Cascadia got a hook in Tahoma guide the populace into sage cleansings & cappucinos. Clouds moved in, whole farms of 'em, colored the sunset salmon, apricot & lavender but only a horizon slice before darkness, bright fire to bounce off Bellevue glass rebound off Lake Xacuabš become (for a minute) (for me & Brenda) a door (yes, liberation) just this side Hillman City the spot where she & I "I did" each other & so far we do & so far we are & w/ Ella here who knows where the scatting takes us or who'll be there in our Sowilo-tinted vision field. How manage the ethical principles define the value-neutral will force?

Sound of crow's caw
didn't liberate blossoms
but sure looked like it.

9:05A – 6.18.12

72

69. Go Dolly Go!
(Goodbye Lakes Aldwell & Mills)

When the neighbor puts on her vacuum cleaner, it sucks up all our ideas.

—Ramón Gomez de la Serna

When the Elwha Dam and the Glines Canyon Dam were blowed up the strait sucked out the first of a century of stopped up sediment. Sediment plume paints the straight gray, frees five species of Pacific salmon. Puts the shine back on the Elwha Snowfinger, diamonds revealed in the rock garden. Lake Aldwell & Lake Mills, filed with the rest of settler prehension.

The historic slack waters of Lake Aldwell are changing to a delta environment with swift water conditions. River channels with steep banks are changing rapidly, are unpredictable, and hazardous to visitors. Access around the remaining reservoir is therefore closed to vehicle, bicycle, foot traffic, and boating.

Elwha Dam, 1910 – 2011
Glines Canyon Dam, 1927 – 2012

Dear Dolly Varden,
    follow the gray to the end
then turn left.

10:48 – 7.17.12

73

70. The Return of the Elwha King

If fish sang we should have to keep them in cages and then they would die because the water would all come out.

—Ramón Gomez de la Serna

The King is Back! Blue-green & silver-sided repository of Omega 3's *Oncorhynchus tshawytscha*. One hundred years later he had no scroll left by Grandpa. She had no treasure map left by Grandma. They had no GPS to re-find the lost land behind Elhwa dams & 150 days after the dams were sent back to hell; 150 days after the long delayed blasts (one small step for man, one giant leap for Chinook Salmon); 150 days after they done blowed up what aughtn't a been there anyway, the King returns.

He's back!

& needed to feed all those Cracker Climate Refugees whose Texas crude's burning all creation. He's back! Belly full of planktonic diatoms, copepods, kelp, seaweed, jellyfish, starfish, bugs, amphipods & crustaceans so delicious served up at Sakura as sake or sakekama w/ side of Mu poured by Sam.

He's back. The King found his pitchflare/prepares herself for the banquet & the initiatory forge long foretold.

> Welcome to Cascadia
> climate refugees. Leave yr religion
> back in the flatland   & don't forget
> to say   *grace.*

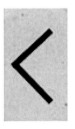

9:13am – 8.22.12

74

71. The Ambassador From Bakersfield
(for Robert Duncan)

One cloud up there is being chased by the police.

—Ramón Gomez de la Serna

& then the swarm of night bees gone from the hive   part of the soul of
the Ambassador from Venus from whose heart the fire master wd return
to, wd occasionally grant permission words compressd, language avails
itself (co-creator of rimes) *a tone leading of vowels* vowels known to be the
soul of the poem, consonants, the body.
                                        & the body there to be purgatoried
night after night a tone leading to breakdown of kidneys (abandonment
fear maybe) or beat abandonment to the gate, always a vast, hatted, middle
aged woman to appreciate such tones to appreciate (not repetition)
emphasis *so that speech may come when the mind is not yours* & certainly not
Ramón's (but maybe his) maybe that of the cloud, the bee swarm, the off-
beach sea stacks that hack at another Pacific wave or the stars themselves
finding amusement in their slow path to the first planet past Venus.

You can't take a piss ... w/o getting hit by a myth but what myths are
made by assignation after assignation what karma's bought for a handful
of essence what what what what what what is only part of what Stellar
Jay might say getting his bird jag on in forests this side of Ruby Beach,
the rain forest before rain season the eyes looking at you while looking
three rows behind you & the stars burning a hole in the ink of the Hoh
night sky.

          In the outlands of the sun's
                              decline, let us
          reconvene *The Symposium of the Whole*,
                    leave not even
                              one working bee.

                                        9:31P – 10.9.12
                                        Rainforest Hostel, Forks, WA

75

72. Moss Spruce Cedar Cathedral

The glitter of her jewels illustrates the ambition of her thoughts.

—Ramón Gomez de la Serna

The shine of the orca's teeth illustrates the animacy of his intentions. The ovoid of his eye outlines a smile for salmon, eagle, chief & raven. The raven's throaty caw settles in the soft fur of the licorice fern or in that of the clubmoss festoons branches of the ancient Olympic vine maple.

Here we can imagine rocks as being thrilled (enthralled) by the current of the memory of events. Here we can see a fish in his dorsal fin, a salmon on her back, a chief with headdress just behind the eyes. Here, her moss spruce cedar cathedral the king travels only after waiting for the rainrainrain or the final dam crash. Here the glaciers had the last say raven wingbeats plot ritmo espíritual sea stacks choke off another pacific wave, the runes predict travel and lavender and blood.

Here, more than dirt
dance floor of ancestors
now unbound.

8:29P – 10.10.12
Rainforest Hostel, Forks, WA

73. Ode to Sun Mask

The moon and the sun have only one bed between them, so one has to work while the other sleeps.

–Ramón Gomez de la Serna

Sun up there he was right in your face w/ his face & his teeth a solar grill in a grimace aiming for dogwood & sun down the moon's up, a Raven Moon a Rainforest Moon a Frost Moon a moon about to be bearded. & the sun again again he rises w/ talons of gold and red and black tentacles edging out from a solar corona creating form from behind a mask of yellow cedar & cedar bark & rope & acrylic just in time to burn something or start to hit the other side of the candle wick or to become a twilight hymn again, hymn to awakening, hymn to Black Rivers (*Rios Negros*) & they shine & he still up, sun yeah, & eyes wide open still a mouth fat on a disc or heat or a dream, dream of the grass blowing east against the source of the still up sun or a dream of getting the ball to curve up or in, a sort of migraine cathedral built with trumpet or other horns built with a sense of inherent bebop which you thought was a song of the night but there it comes bright as day until it's dying for a nap a nap while it's still bright out but its nap is our night & the moon, she gotta get up & out, gotta get a shine on she got to take off that flannel & become more ee haichka-like two arms up, palms in but open & she gotta let owl back into latihan she gotta get ready for the backscratch she gotta dig clams & smoke fish because no one knows when the tsunami's going to come, no one knows when the Elwha starts running back unsiltifying itself, no one knows when to stop running & start thinking about September again & the advent of avalanche fields & the trail that would be here now gone down there to the realm of dental records, past the ripe blue & thimbleberries down where the blood is & the bruxism & the river gods quiet enough & you can hear 'em there beside the flat stones. Me & Rebecca did. Stone eyes & straw hair & some'd be beret'd & some would look like Lester Bowie & til the day they take her away or they take you away & everyone will run out of salt but the sun & the moon have their arrangement & everybody got to get some sleep sometime.

Yr just scrapin off last year's plums
from the apron
      when the Lady sings
         Do it agin.

7:234P – 10.11.12
Rainforest Hostel, Forks, WA

74. The Use of Wunjo

The stag is the son of tree and lightning.

—Ramón Gomez de la Serna

Start the day free of dreamtime with the knowing that the tendons ought remember how to bend again full range of their multiverse how the runes might include Wunjo how a candle burns for it in honor of it, to prolong *power and bliss and buildings good enough.*

Good enough to find a rainforest in which to retreat to honor a Duncan Cedar or moss hall or just be an ambassador from Slaughter still searching   (searching) for the antidote that may need to be released from the tendons searching w/o pressing, not to be depressed by *hands, power, looks, diligence, art, blossom,* greengage plums & stolen asian pears. (They weren't being used.) Use is honor Maximus knew.

& what's the use of a rune bag never sees a non-dominant hand the use of a rune which'd warn you of danger but not be heeded why can't they always be Wunjo & washed up walking sticks that got Hoh writ all over 'em? Wunjo as the result of wisdom & good rep, living sin temor, never misusing the imagination w/ mindfotos of doom.

Dream write yoga prayer divination facebook baby cry breakfast email email email.

New idea of stag
            party – wash dishes
      fill up water filter.

9:30A – 10.18.12

79

75. Translating the Digital Fire
(For Dharma Mitra)

When you say "asterisks" it is like speaking of tiny pieces of a star.

—Ramón Gomez de la Serna

& each tiny piece breaks off as a person, punctuation as person, Sister Comma, Uncle Semicolon & Brother Mitra tending the digital fire from which the sutras are situated & he, like the sea salt farmer filtering from the ash of a foreign language what may be of use as a door of liberation or maybe a basement window how the transformation skillful how burn the hatefulness & delusion though only as ornery as grabbing the collar of the glass-eyed demon for a face punch or 5.

> Namo Guanyin Bodhisattva
> Namo Guanyin Bodhisattva
> Namo Guanyin Bodhisattva

one hundred eight bead-festooned times. How a spider on the car flap headed for your head no doubt to burrow and lay eggs a door of liberation as much as the harvested octopus not so deep in Puget Sound Cove 2 as to not hear the   c l a n g   of metal rods & then a fist fight for a college art project to be drawn & then drawn and quartered & dinner.

Give me the black walnut thud on pavement or the sound of the gentle rainrainrain on Que's windshield its own liberation door of silent light inconceivable. Give me the bountiful season's last November raspberry. Neighbors have had their fill. Six more are undefiled. The stars are polished off my boots. The digital fire roars on no one needs to fix it.

> Fire in pixels. Fire
>   on the boveda. Fire's
> how the ancestors get your attention.

8:41A – 11.5.12

Protecting sea life in Puget Sound

Some areas of Puget Sound are off limits to fishing. The killing of an octopus off Alki Point -- an unprotected area -- has sparked a call for a new state Marine Protected Area.

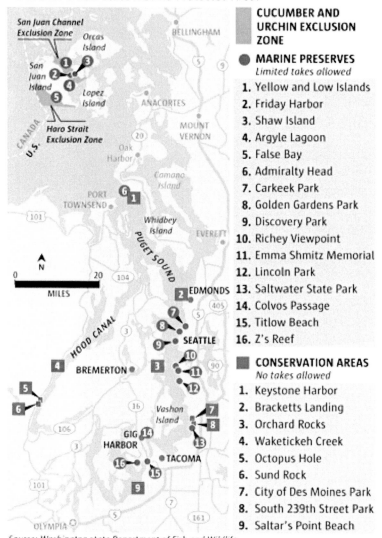

CUCUMBER AND URCHIN EXCLUSION ZONE

● **MARINE PRESERVES**
Limited takes allowed

1. Yellow and Low Islands
2. Friday Harbor
3. Shaw Island
4. Argyle Lagoon
5. False Bay
6. Admiralty Head
7. Carkeek Park
8. Golden Gardens Park
9. Discovery Park
10. Richey Viewpoint
11. Emma Shmitz Memorial
12. Lincoln Park
13. Saltwater State Park
14. Colvos Passage
15. Titlow Beach
16. Z's Reef

■ **CONSERVATION AREAS**
No takes allowed

1. Keystone Harbor
2. Bracketts Landing
3. Orchard Rocks
4. Waketickeh Creek
5. Octopus Hole
6. Sund Rock
7. City of Des Moines Park
8. South 239th Street Park
9. Saltar's Point Beach

Source: Washington state Department of Fish and Wildlife

MARK NOWLIN / THE SEATTLE TIMES

76. Ode to Snowberry (or Madrone)

The trouble is that evergreens are everdead.

—Ramón Gomez de la Serna

& so depend on foliage (it's all in the accessorizing) how a few red berries hang from the madrone from Tofino to Santa Barbara (madroño) with leaves can last four years. Red berries known to hitch their barbs to northbound elk. Branches known to contort and twist aim for a certain star, blossoms confused with constellations.

But snowberry forms (waits) soon all's barren but the everdead, soon salal, Oregon grape have a say but snowberry in winter ornaments the view this side Tahoma awaits a white-tail or grouse. This common snowberry with an inflorescence (16 flowers). This common snowberry with almost a glow at night watches the windmade Lake Xacuabš waves as the baby does.

You might say *everdead* Ramón but bust open a snowberry for the delicate hexagonal within. Few so bright can stand the contrast can hide from predators can wait as patient as madroño for fire to circulate the seed.

   Oh snowberry
      the favorite barren winter
  drupe...
     hang on.

5:03P – 12.5.12
4817 S Lucile B

82

77. Clean Shirt (It Never Entered My Mind)

All nice mornings wear a clean shirt.

—Ramón Gomez de la Serna

& all nice December Cascadia mornings wear flannel, layers & no umbrella, strive not for thinking or for not thinking but for without-thinking (take a kind attitude toward your lack of thoughts). Here, pure presence, hear things as they are. Here moss grows fat on the walk, greens the wood stairs. Here an hostile takeover just so slow no one notices.

Without-thinking neither affirms nor denies, accepts nor rejects, believes nor disbelieves... an unobjectified presence... a non-conceptual or prereflective mode of consciousness Kasulis says of the Zen of Dogen who says

Because reality/Hardly seems real/Why assume/That dreams/Are really dreams? May be ongoing presences or the madroño reaches out another inch for a slice of the widening December Cascadia sun. May be the movement of moss up the stoop steps or the green of the winter madrone leaves hide behind red berries or at least your prehension of it (fully penetrated) the cultivation of surrender's what he might've been after the quivering hand made to quiver by a presence controll'd by someone (thing?) else, same as it always is when prehended (apprehended) by the force superior always gets another record on (sin aire muerto) maybe Miles this time *It Never Entered My Mind* trumpet mourning that you're not *there again to get into my hair again* or so it would be sung in the dream/not dream where one is not not thinking but without-thinking again (prehending) -- a clean flannel shirt. And every 5:27 you re-cue Miles & Trane, Mr. PC, Red & Philly Joe & they go again as in 1956 because the dream has no end if you are with out thinking & it's no dream.

Thinking about not thinking
dirties the shirt. Wait
'til there's no

thing   here

11:12P – 12.26.12
4817 S Lucile B

78. Wren & Whale Surrender

*One who drinks through a straw is becoming a bird and there is a moment towards
the end of summer when he succeeds.*

—Ramon Gomez de la Serna

Could be a wren (Ah-up-wha-eek) atop the Nuu-chah-nulth whale
translates whale behavior to the whale hunter not in accordance with
the unity of the plan *heshook-ish tsawalk*. All in the whaling canoe true to
protocols *cleansed, purified… in harmony*. You can up the volume of your
songs, can wonder   (as whale tows you out to sea) what might've escaped
order 'til wren as messenger (again) *the little brown bird* whispers: *Tell the
whale to go back where it was harpooned.*

Later you find protocol
broken back at home when one heard whale'd taken the harpoon and
whale, sensing the deal breached, headed to sea. Later you find your songs
enough to attract an intermediary (a go-between) could translate whale
speak into Nuu-chah-nulth. Much later you find you're simply a prisoner
in the *Dictatorship of Reason* – spirit, appetite, faith, emotion, intuition,
imagination, experience all stuffed in the back of the empirical canoe. (It's
all methodology.)

In the department store, some
one must move the mannequins
& haul in basketball hoops.

Threes to shoot a *spiritual primacy to existence* how a bear in a dream smiles,
teeth 4 to 5 inches long could be sent to surrender his body/teach the
querent *how to make medicine.* You could make a method (poetry?) in which
make up for the *sort of cultural and psychic lobotomy* any sons of settlers've
suffered.

Your life, career that
daily latté but a shadow of a reality
of the show the Divine (through Wren)
conspires for those in surrender.

7:16A – 1.7.13
4817 S Lucile B

79. Kano and The Snake

As far as the stars are concerned, we are always in a bottomless pit.

—Ramon Gomez de la Serna

In a bottomless pit in a Snake Year in the Year of the Water Snake yin to last year's Dragon yang. What will be done this year, will be revealed this year as snakes and their ilk pick vibes like nobody's business ilk pick or resonances of the ancestors under yr bootsoles & do you make your own ancestors live or let them dish you up a tendon at a time?

Can Kano (Kenaz) find enough light for a late uncle to pass along a lipful of alliteration, can Kenaz be a "signpost in the navigation of the ancestral stream" do what we can to hiss and tell in this Water Snake year, do what Lincoln did, or Mao or other snakes like Oprah? Yes, this snake is black, this snake is female, this snake contains mainly fire.

Pearl Harbor, Tiananmen Square & September 11 all Snake Year events. My last daughter was born a dragon, not a snake. But a sister snake (and an Aries) and a snake of wood at that. Science, tech, research, education all love a snake year, but a water snake year a black water snake year?

Here, in the bottomless pit
we call earth
we fatten the snake, ask
ancestors
help us hold the venom.

8:39A – 1.27.13

80. Ian Boyden's Bear Dream Bird Dream
(For Ian on his 102nd Birthday)

The sea is the oldest rotary press in the world, incessantly printing in retrogravure
<u>*The Daily Wave*</u>.

—Ramon Gomez de la Serna

In the dance to understand what a man is he made his head out of bird
seed, dreaming head cast of seed in yellow with black bits *let me pick your
brain* they might say if they could say something beyond *tweet* if they could
beat the feast spread out for raccoons, cats, ants, slugs. Instead of your name
(mis-spelled) adorning a *calle* some day, here he wd watch his head cast in
seed be eaten by a bunch of birds or a dancing bear who'd paw it and lick
it and mix it maybe with berries. He'd found a man's head so impermanent
& what is left but bear shit or bird shit & some ghostly resonances on the
walls, some descendant or poet of the future picks up in waves or an inspired
bit of metaphor.

      & here he cd   he cd make his head of concrete, ape
the acts of those who seek the immortal & pigeon roosts   & pitch it in
the rushing spring river for 100 meters of rapids to render it nest stuff for
salmon beds, 100 meters all she needs, she who is permeable, she who
gathers armies of compassion this water bodhisattva so soft so ready to
surrender & eat Ian's concrete head in 100 rushing meters.

      In the dance
to understand what a man is   (in one last dance) he'd stock a pond w/
carp & more concrete heads of his, fish food in eye holes & nose holes &
mouth − carp as visiting immortals he thinks − swam here from Penglai
− (ichthiomorphism) fish-centric & if we could fool the immortals for a
moment, what wisdom wd they have for us? & if we could see paradise as
our highest/deepest wish. & if the fish could wish & kiss & whisper what
would our concrete head hear & wonder & what wd be left, & what would
that have to say?

      In the dance to understand
        what a man is how
    does he treat women, how
          do animals/children dance
      to the sound of his name?

               9:17A − 2.16.13

81. Moonbank (After Xi Chuan)

The moon is a failed bank of metaphors.

—Ramon Gomez de la Serna

Yet there in the night, the Beijing sky counts the dead, halts to hear our *primal cries* elk skulls whiten by her headlights, footprints of those who'd travel the cosmos astonished by the her & the poem which *identifies its writer to the world, but only… when the writer… is out of the way.* & the writer tries to stay out the eyes of black cats out the eyes of seagulls scattered by downtown helicopters, out the eyes of the babushka'd woman, who'd notice them noticing her on a night trades its moon for March grays.

But the dead the dead still announce their presence, not so much as wind or white smoke, more as salmon find their way back to spawning gravel by riverbank, as friend to moon or moon assistant (moon confidant) as wave who helps the moon beam to the right characters in the city night, silent-like as if always there ready to illuminate the cage we find our way into & out of. Moon – the poet's subject – as Time is. Moon as funereal, sinister, regenerative when reflected off water, holding (as are we all) holding off the waning. Sol y Luna, alma y cuerpo, El Rey y Soltera de Agua (the happy couple) because she the woman knows she will never die so hears cries primal, whitens eye holes of elk skulls, she counts shades.

She the failed bank won't tank the economy, she too big to fail with the soul of an animal as the seat of sensation. She sends snow, hears all cries, she might wander but widdershins and rises with chariot speed could there be a more bella bodhisattva in the night sky?

> *Don't wait*
> > the poet says
> > > *till the moon drills*
> *holes into you.* The Moon she's got
> > > > yr back.

4:48P – 3.13.13

82. Automedicador
(For Amalio)

He had his fortune invested in sheets, but one day he was robbed by a platoon of ghosts.

—Ramon Gomez de la Serna

Turn Back! What's an automedicador w/o his pocket insulin? What's Garcia doing in the forsythia, why Garcia under the Chinese Witch Hazel bush, puzzled by the Arboretum's Camper Down Elm? Garcia on acid for a week, a month, a year melting the walls of his brain maybe or just turning doors of perception into bliss and windows.

The legends of Garcia grow (still after the elusive metaphor) down by the river where he got his free sandals where he watches his step aware of Corua by the Embudo where it stripes itself with the Big River. Garcia eyeing the waitresses, ordering tuna tataki or sending tulips to the Lady of the house always to ward off the confusion of all sentient beings' erroneous views, *usually projection* Garcia sings, part Yaqui, part Jung, part Chinese, eating Crispy Pimp with Jidi Majia in Xining.

Garcia stabs himself w/ another needle for the hit of a warm hormone & regulate his fat metabolism stabb'd smack dab the middle of the island of his Yaqui belly without even an ouch and more than a pinch of gratitude. Garcia an oxy for his hip, a smile in his eye under the full blossom'd Cascadia cherry tree on that rare March day. Holy Garcia laughing laughing his hoarse man ghost laugh w/ overgrown ear hair.

> The ghosts'll come
> one day, but not to
> day. Today Garcia
> orders one more Dragon
> roll.

1:12P – 4.1.13

83. Buddha Diet

Buddha is the only religious founder never went on a diet.

—Ramon Gomez de la Serna

but still stunned in March by the rapid ascent of magnolia blossoms, *scattering jewels in all directions*. Fascinated by bootcrunch of stairway catkins that stay'd firm 'til April rain. Reborn as a baby w/ joy to kick legs again, joy dance in the kitchen to Beck's *Qué Onda Guero* bounce to *Guatemalan soccer ball instant replay*. Hear the transmission of rhythm, here joy embodied, a future tool to *evaporate oceans of cravings* he wanted to say w/ *clear eyes & deep understanding* only slightly addled by Mu   drunk with the orphaned son of an illiterate carnival fry cook.

Still stunn'd by the snowless winter the stolen alley jasmine wd perfume the home dance floor for a week, bounce to the joy of baby's eighth dance *Qué Onda Guero*, Buddha somewhere eating ribs from Jones bbq w/ *clear eyes revealing the treasury of non-regressing great compassion* for the pig who wanted a taste of the Buddha while stolen magnolia blossoms unfurl /explode into reluctant April, another *wheel of teaching in reality like space*. Kick Kick Kick fat baby legs define joy in meat & tendons signified by a five toothed smile. The hymn of the Indian Plum still echoes off the corridor walls. We'll remember soon where lilac trees hid all winter & she may remember how, en L.A. español to say *what's up gangster? en un ritmo perfecto. Qué Onda Guero.*

        From gangster
            to winter kale gardener
        mimic the Buddha's
            disdain for dieting.

8:43P – 4.8.13

84. Hold the House Sparrow
(For Maleea Acker)

A real civilization would invent messenger seagulls.

—Ramon Gomez de la Serna

& prefer the enormous face of the Snake King or the Northern Flicker at the birdfeeder, feted by House Finches but please no House Sparrows at this house. How would a real civilization deal with Starlings, House Sparrows, other invaders? Let natural selection unfurl under the feeder?

She wd find a box, a trap for House Sparrow. She, not squeamish having helped her own Pop gut fish on the dock, she wd take this box, this trap, catch these critters unwanted & smash 'em between two blocks of firewood, a clean kill. A prairie re-born in her backyard. An immigrant neighbor incensed at how she'd refuse lawns, roundup & other addictions specific to bourgeois conformity & snuff the pint-sized invaders.

Without question the most deplorable event in the history of American ornithology was the introduction of the English Sparrow & she'd agree "winged rats" attack bluebirds, peck holes in their skulls. How such a gentle culture (HA!) release such demons? Drop 'em in New Zealand, find 'em in Hawaii. Put 'em in a Northern Flicker lover's backyard and find 'em flattened 'tween two pieces of firewood, liberated w/ great compassion.

Out the beak
of the House Sparrow no "philip."

Barely a peep.

9:01A – 4.19.13

85. Soul's Same Ol' (Over n Over)
(For Walter Davis Jr. After Nate Mackey)

Nothing saddens a child more than realizing the merry-go-round is beginning to slow down.

—Ramon Gomez de la Serna

& so he'd call himself Solito, as if soul were ordinary, as if soul were same ol' same ol' & beyond the leash of reason he might say, or she might as in the first perception the wheel lost velocity. He might have not sd *soul* but instead sd "jiwa" & it'd be one and the same same ol' same ol'. It'd be the respite or the dance devised the moment the Charlie Christian riff come on the box. It'd be the laugh in the baby's eyes as the dance starts or leg kick she enacts to whip cracks of Lene Lovich in the moment when she declaims her Lucky Number as "one."

So, Solito it'd be but soul goes on, non-local like. What next? Movement. Meat lever activated as latihan engages. Here's a left shoulder shudder, shrugging it all off. Here a right hand imagines magic navigating waves or waving in the April wind. & so goes the simple life of what soul is. Solito, he'd say & then get Walter Davis Jr. on the box for *Off Minor*, ninety-one seconds of mirth. *Off Minor* over & over & over & when it slows, get back on the wheel (hit repeat) because we continue to be stunned by its orbit, stunned by the amount of sun comes through in 1.5 minutes, stunned to have such soul stuck on the radio w/ a hundred seconds before NPR news headlines, get one last plunk to *petition the mythic through the ether* he might've sd, slogging to get beyond "a surrender with the will..." Get to "a surrender aimed [at] the life within."

But Monk (sans circles) aimed for this, Walter Davis Jr. too aimed that way, way of jiwa of self unbound therefore cd never be lonely, but by leaving behind Evin, Alana, Sareenah & Alicia & at least nighty-one seconds of jiwa-deepening mirth cd brace us for the latest Crime, Sports, Weather & Whatever.

Plunk away
Walter Davis Jr.

yr way beyond
some Godforsaken interval.

12:03A – 4.30.13

91

86. Paulownia Tomentosa

His "Good Day!" was always overcast.

—Ramon Gomez de la Serna

& yes, he was from Seattle. & yes, the sun was shining that particular Friday in the season of lilac blossoms and full bloom Empress Tree, Princess Tree, *Paulownia tomentosa*, stolen from central and western China but an invader here loving the lack of competition for what sun there is, shaping purple hanging bell blossoms and leaves in pairs. We sit under it, take fotos, are there if we think about it, Lakewood Park.

& by *good day* he meant, in Seattle nice, courtesy and not much else, will wait for your street crossing, will not honk, "a city of the mind . . . a city of geeks. People here . . . totally blow you off" the newcomer'd say in The Times. But not at the stop sign beyond the Empress Tree. Not at the four way stop where *you go no you go no you go* & the guy from Chicago goes knowing your M.O., knowing driving the car "is personality enshrined."

& overhead's a helicopter shopping for dark-skinned shooting suspects & here the "anti-capitalism May Day riots" only 3 businesses w/ busted windows & here a view of deep Elliott Bay azul under snow-capped Olympics seeking a hearing. *Good day*, always overcast, always an undertone, somewhere the intimacy's obscured. Some know the names of dogs at the dog park but not the ones the other side of the leash. Not the neighbor's name or wife, but their latté order or wifi-signal & how much in their compost bin. Is it the weather? Topography? It is a "social script that leads to alienation" but Emmett Watson didn't want you here anyway and we can't make a left on Denny at 1:40 in the afternoon & bike-riders forego single file just to hack at you & your humongous carbon footprint. In Slaughter I once saw a yard sign that said simply: "Vote No!" Can whip it out for any election. *Vote No*, democracy easy as yard signs & being against. (Just put a line through it.) Easy as stopping for one pedestrian or take a pill or cut it out, or the bombing starts in 5 minutes or the settler prehension a century after the perimeter's secured.

& yes, the sun shines that particular Friday the season of late magnolia blossoms, of English Heather or Scotch Broom petals sticking their heads out of leaves this side the highway, season of lilac blossoms & the full bloom Empress Tree, Princess Tree.

Paulownia tomentosa,
stolen from western China
but just an invader here
like you & me.

3:00P – 5.3.13
@ Louisa's

87. Help from the Heavens

When he is home, the astronomer always keeps looking up at the ceiling.

—Ramon Gomez de la Serna

For a falling sky. For an obsolete constellation brought back to service. For the threshold of heat-trapping gasses in the atmosphere (400 ppm) for the first time in 3 million years since our last bout of anthropocentric hubris only a pole shift cd sweeten.

Here, at Bertschi Elementary, hard rain makes rainwater gush through the classroom, make a woooooshing sound, make a met Living Building Challenge where rainwater's dumped no more, where 5th graders monitor energy use, consult with 4th graders, get the debit card to buy more solar panels. Stare at the ceiling of a Living Building. Treat Gaia as a series of inter-connected bioregions vie for the race to return to use what you need, seek redress again.

Here World War III - 1st world war which the world's not a theater, but actor, test the fact of animism, that the biggest one of all might have a sucker punch for House Sparrows, capitalists and fume-spewers.

> O master of the universe
> give us back the Print Shop, the Slug
> or the Mussel. We may need help here
> sent from the Heavens.

9:25A – 5.13.13

94

88. Lesser Quantico

When we take a bath we always drown a few of our memories.

—Ramón Gomez de la Serna

& Robin would've migrated north to Vancouver by this time set in Cascadia ready to vet the *real that is Jack's concern.* For even when dead (ever when dead) catch up w/ the I that was he to *use it then to lose it* (almost typed *love.*) *No heat or torment realizes this.*

             Can stash a whistleblower in the bowels of Marine hell (Quantico) – isolate him 23 of 24 hours, take away blankets, glasses, sleep, clothes, exercise, can hope resolve (& hope)'d wither w/ muscles but make a martyr out of him see what you do to future generations that can sniff out a war criminal from here, patriot?

                  So the open then (the serial) *an attack on the "subjective aim" and assurance of a whole culture*, a whole poetry unwrapped from personality – a bigger fish here for the pan. Canning spontaneity same consciousness as the rehearsed trial, same consciousness as the culture that's an anti-culture manufactured (like consent) by Disney n' Nikon (or Nike) and not the real like soup

                               or used prams left on street corners for parents w/o such means, p-patch kale flowers the Hmong farmer'd fry w/ garlic & olive oil or those first local cherries of the season. The real which never gets to Quantico or those stuck in quanticos of their own making. *A reopened language lets the unknown, the Other, the outside in again as a voice in the language* but we worked so hard to get to the top of the food chain (brain chain) as it were, not just to give control to someone (thing) we cain't even see!

    Don't wash out the memories
 w/ the water boards,
     citizen. They may be
         gaining on you.

              12:11P – 6.4.13

89. Pocket Fetch

Sunflowers: pocket-mirrors of the sun.

—Ramón Gomez de la Serna

& sunflowers are seen in the City of Big Shoulders where stinking onions & sewers rushing after the rain punctuate the humid summer air. & sunflowers do not have much in the way of shoulders yet look at those September heads filled w/ seed the squirrel hunts climbing up the stalk stealing a peek in the pocket mirror & not everyone can shoulder the burden they think they might, eyes bigger than their shoulders the fetch lurks somewhere near here to take on a task or twenty.

Ehwaz is the rune of the psycho-spiritual construct called the Fetch. Your Fetch is the opposite gender as you, inactive in the material plane but still quite accessible within your spirit...

Fetching, indeed.
Forget the stick, fetch a few Franklins because baby needs a new Z4 Roadster. Baby needs a new house & garden full of fourteen foot high sunflowers mirror the abundant Cascadia sun. Baby needs parents can roadtrip her to Grandma's, load up on español, sopa de frijoles negros y picadillo, y arroz Ai!

So, you await the next thunderstorm,
secure the services of a Blood Hawk (totem) & hoarse your voice in support of the Blackhawks, you try to find the watermark of the visit/secure your own shoulders in the upright and locked position, fully aware the maximum weight they bear, fully aware the role of the fetch, far from libido no matter how many dreams of finger-fucking you have, fully aware that family's there & your's is a sunflower, a little grimy, always near the railroad, mostly unaware of the function of the fetch beyond a wily labrador. The DNA may be dormant.

The polis is constellated
around the sun
(she says).   Fetch that slice of DNA not
a curse.

9:13A – 6.24.13
1903 W Argyle, Apt 3
Chicago, IL

90. Slow Down Tahoe Driver
(For Brian Love)

Our only real property consists of our bones.

—Ramón Gomez de la Serna

A hard way for the orbit to expand, the car crash & instant death after Independence Day. Bones & a hat they'd rescue from the spot where Auburn Way North becomes Auburn Way South, a crawl from the Rainbow bar, hard way for one's orbit to expand. A spot on the parade route. How your baritone'd call out each float, each entry, each Good Ol' Day moving outhouse rolls west on Main in Slaughter right there during the season of the Ripe Plum Full Moon, slow enough to practice the religion of plum blossoms unaware here's where the Tahoe'd blow through the red & blow a hole in our lives in one last t-bone. & the sunset the night you died, I know, Doc, I know, maybe I apply something angelic to rays affix themselves to clouds over West Hill. Maybe it's me projecting a need to see you've crossed over safe to be reunited with your speed & the Supreme Barber in the sky will cut off that god-forsaken beard, pour you a Scotch and water, wait for a story about the cross-eyed prize bull at the Puyallup Fair.

Ilalqo's where waters come together, each stream unique to itself surrenders to a larger current, becomes something more than they'd be alone, one of those vortexes were local tribes'd stop & linger, so slow they'd be, so deliberate. & there you'd be dubbing old Art Pepper cds, maybe listening to *The Trip*,   the prison tale of stories told behind bars so ride the imagination for a while, a respite from the cell. Bones, Doc. That's all we own anyway & yours, how much longer could they take you inhaling cigars or any more Scotch anyway? We'd have wished for one last goodbye.

> Slow Down Tahoe Driver.
> You never know whose brother's
> on the other side.

8:27A – 7.7.13

91. Berber City Poems
(For El Habib Louai)

There are railway stars, shining near stations, which give out more cold than other stars.

—Ramón Gomez de la Serna

In the book of Berber, there may be an August nasturtium, a postcard garden, a walking salad & portrait of the young poet as José Lezama Lima ensuring his *alma no esta en un cenicero*. There would be a Hillman City hummingbird somewhere behind Desolation & the stolen word of the day might be *eggs* or *Amtrak*. Lenin aside, there would be homage almost everywhere you'd go in this leap, this certain Ripe Plum Moon moment this certain lack of asides, this tour of famous graves.

                       & you'd become a Berber too, you'd find rare Baranda epigraphs & etch them into dirt beyond anthills, wd try to find a stolen kind of taste & be content   to plant the garden / wait to see what volunteers pop up in a year, what mambo steps the baby masters by next time, write your way through August, through postcards, past the last chair in the p-patch, always making new aside the ghost of Robin Blaser.

                     To be a Berber in the city means time, means blossoms, means the cat must mambo through the urban forest, means huckleberries slow the long slog up the Peak to where Jack's shack beckons, warming railway stars whose beams link Cascadia and cities named for saints, means the art of how a cherry tomato links the dark sounds of the dream & jiwa & J.J. Cale, all inside a blackness worn as a mask of fat. Reuben sandwiches & wasabi moments with Sam. Mu for you, but not for a Muslim.

                   Find yrself
                        as a city Berber for a
           fortnight, how measure the vigil
                 keeps one irregular?

                                         9:34A – 9.14.13

92. Galactic Circuit
(for Will Alexander)

The snail is always ascending its own staircase.

—Ramón Gomez de la Serna

& will alexander, the **G**alactic runaway, the *transposed coronal*
Al*geria* – "reading and losing [him]self in the process" of [perhaps] lighting
the candle from the bLack widow's love cake or a five spot laid @ the grave of
his **A***kashic precursors* to *cancel* [his] *structureless sCrutiny* [signed up here for as
much as i Can chew] **t**he   "sTutterings
of dolphy and vallejo"
    Insinuating
           trails of **C**omets

                through the **C**osmos' lesser-traveled
realms, eaten from the **I**nside out our own less than rapid oxidation [he'd
say *astRal   oblitertation   maybe*]'d say *furious   obduradtion*   con   una
Cara seria, say *all the aromas were suspended* as *the body is eaten as*
vapoUr. & so goes the *biokinetIc elevation* [aspiration] "these things begIn to
whisper/insinuate
Themselves."

           Fellow galactic traveler
      Will Alexander, for whose study we forego
         crib notes for
             star charts

    we'll assure your *own hosannahs*
              resound.

6:04A – 9.29.13

99

93. The Fog Wet Web

Smoke never quite manages to scribble a mustache on the sky.

—Ramón Gomez de la Serna

Nothing takes weight of October fog more serious than spider webs.
October 23, 2013.

& they'll take it for a fogmageddon fortnight & no more, the last drying line left in the neighborhood drying what might be diamonds for your mind   only because the fog covers all / illuminates color rampant in October Cascadia of maybe rose hips   or the grass coming back or the Irish Strawberry Tree now the culprit of the seemingly broomless neighbor on the way to PCC.

    & it'll be *fogmageddon* says Cliff Mass, "An extraordinary persistent ridge of high pressure over the eastern Pacific and West Coast" for which a large soy almond latté may stand in as an attempted antidote, but for the spider, an October fly's a rare slice of meat more likely a rose petal or recent maple leaf & the web's bejeweled & heavy with serious weight of summer's sins still staining late October. The Cascadia sky unmustached, must settle for yet another chin beard – may the playoffs be over soon – & take the Teahadists with you.

        Here's where we can
            wear the fog.
     Something else spider
                reminds us of.

            7:20A – 10.25.13

94. Dilettante Periphery

Nothing is repeated: it just <u>looks</u> similar.

—Ramón Gomez de la Serna

& here at The Lake (Graves built) sunslip past cedartops that side tiny lichen-festooned islands & w/ yr head a certain angle here are "instruments for a new navigation." Monet sd a finished work of art an "unreasonable pretension" & this unfinished work's Cascadia's Giverny more a monument to solitude (practice of inside) & grove of Grandfather trees date from the late T'ang era. No. Tourists. Ever.

"The dilettante periphery has so little to do but keep these things stirred up for their titillation" / won't get the red meat of fotos nor see what light left on this Sunday of the thinnest veil becomes another tiny lichen-festoon'd island. (Iris island.)

Redwood canopy sways
backlit by Cascadia
azul – above Graves'
Lake.

Nothing looks the same as this yearning for an *auspicious wind* / yearndeep to abide *Securely Beyond Obstruction*, a sober puer-fueled invite to the *all pervading light* lit by horsetails & sword ferns, ciananthus & Italian marble, a soft path up & elevate the heart rate. "Here is the heart of this bulletin"

Clover grows in needles
dropped by Redwood trees on
the path to bench three.

& lie there looking up sure NOT to squish a banana slug & cd die there if required – give the dilettante periphery sumtin' to put in their pipe when they cd be re-sounding their own lost twin's broken hosannahs.

Homebuilding as
            enlightenment practice
        while citizens "tweet
& sleep through the wars."

6p – 11.3.13
The Lake
Loleta, CA

03

95. Sending Out Tendrils

Skulls in museums are laughing at their labels.

—Ramon Gomez de la Serna

To label is to control & control is to dominate & who can dominate when that which does not rot wills itself through skulltop out of this "sigh between two mysteries." The Lake painted w/ swirls of duckweed survive wade of single file coots, otter trips seemingly impervious to wavelets, same that mirror Monday morning November Southern Cascadia sun up the tiny island's lichen-festooned Wax Myrtle. (Wax as mask of fat, *contains the life-substance, hence its use in witchcraft. Myrtle as joy, peace, tranquility, happiness, constancy, victory… the feminine principle… a vital essence & transmits the breath of life.* A more apt symbol for the Master of the Lake may never be met.)

& so hang on to the morning duckweed swirl long as we can w/o possession, laugh out the top of our skulls after latihan, break from inane digital demands, product of this "military contaminated age." In its place firs and lichen lichen lichen. Tiny islands of ancestors & cat-tails, consciousness left to manifest as swordfern & sunbreak. Dreadlocks & giant skunk cabbage. A haymocker of a white, functioning, ritual cleanse necessary in the age of hummers & drones, GMOs & narcolepsy.

> a 150 acre paean
> of ancient redwoods, grand firs
> & lichenized wax myrtles
> to "the living vine of my
> nervous system."

In the dream world they want to date your sisters and you want to pee. In the dream world Dominick can pop finger bits into the air to the sound of Curley Howard. In consciousness manifesting as a lake retreat the heart of this bulletin is the occasion of a coot landing beyond horsetails or distant gunfire confirming the world's not had its coming sudden revelation. And we go on, longing for butter, coffee, beer & bioregional animation. And we go on, offerings for the dead of piano hymns & picadillo, telepathic conifers & constellations as bird baths. & we go on improvising one prehension after another here, because he said it's not death the opposite of life, it's time.

This living vine
        sending out tendrils
(invisible)
           like the smoke of my
                well-tended fire.

10:38a – 11.5.13
The Lake
Loleta, CA

96. The Gift

I am rich thanks to all that I cannot afford.

—Ramón Gomez de la Serna

Your entry is a gift & a gift your exit. Try the labyrinth, for instance. Cd function as feedback or divination strategy depends on insistence of the querent/quality of her hymn. Gebo reflects triple gift of Odin: consciousness/ life breath/ form. Cd be life breath manifesting as lichen-tipped conifers & one cd deduce the air be good here. Cd be form manifesting as a visit by Rufous hummingbird to neighborhood horsetails, nature's kind of cursory check-in. Maybe manifesting as a *Portrait of a Residential Schoolboy* how *post-colonial stress syndrome*'s lampooned in turquoise, rust, azul, tan, green, blues y pepsodented teeth. An involuntary offer akin to Odin's self-sacrifice to the World Tree or a whole Wiyot village's World Renewal Ceremony.

A gift's not a bribe to persuade a god, nor a payment, nor to stave off nature's penance. A gift's the joy of non-attachment, unlike the Bezos or any such center for legal larceny. A gift may be a human-eyed hallucination or Redwood autonomy designed to stave off the glass-crash of ancestors lolling behind the tiny island's Wax Myrtle waiting for better weather. Tongue out, ovoid-eyed you can call in Picasso or Geronimo, Chief Seattle, Yeats or Bugs Bunny. Or take a frame drum as halo, but you learn all blood's one, Doc.

In Denmark, call on the Goddess Gefion, sign off w/ plethora of capital X's, same consciousness as what some call sustainability, some survival of the species. Otter will remain. A free-range gift Hosannah of the moment, his dive always unrushed, impeccable & leaves only the simplest ripples. (A lake ritual.) You go out as you come in, a gift.

Gebo in the impeccable silence
& cloud drift of duckweed swirl
infinite Wednesday
Redwood   afternoon.

1:59p – N.6.13
The Lake, Loleta, CA

97. Clues from Hell

Smoke rises to heaven when it ought to descend to hell.

—Ramón Gomez de la Serna

& a heaven's of yr making a home be it the Rock or Careladen, Woodtown or the Lake, Ka'gean or Cloud Nine, Slaughter or a little corner of Hillman City survivable by p-patch. Make it w/ enough care to notice *from the lichen to the day moon.* From the library to the Japanese Maple. From the giant sunflowers to the three steepled cedar points to better weather.

In it & in the chaos of the marked-up books, the three-toed vase, the empty Otokoyama bottles in the recycle bin, clues. To sift through the wreckage one day they'll want clues. Clues to how you ended up next to a fire (well-tended) & clues to the spiritual chase. Clues to the record & direction (for future seekers) & clues to where you hid the Humboldt Fog. Clues cd hide right in front of you as does the sponge plant by the duckweed drift which smears the morning Lake. Clues of cigarette butts & grief.

Old growth Redwood
800 years old
300 feet tall
heard its share
of prayers.

They were always there we'll say, prominent as miniature islands w/ salal, blue huckleberry & dwarfed spruce. Calm as the Lake ripples made by a coot flock landing. Subtle as the woodsmoke rejecting hell in the making of its new home as it courts the morning Cascadia fog. Sincere as autumn bouquets (*sweet little nosegay like*) for every dead stranger in the cemetery made w/ the spirit of *great cobwebs of geese in the sky* & mild-mannered hallucinations of reverse snow in September Olympic Fireweed or the hush of dropping fir needles w/ each new exhale from Blue Glacier.

So stock up on cake mix & tequila, butter & turkey bacon. Mangoes y pan de banana. Have handy jasmine rice & altar candles, fresh garlic & olive oil. Cashew bits & blush wine. Wool socks & binoculars. Photos of the loved ones & always the clue-enabling ancestors.

Decoding the sea
      & the heavens
   ain't for sissies.
            Lend a hand
                    or stand back.

4:08p – N.8.13
The Lake
Loleta, CA

98. Why Redwings Sing

Moonbeams always manage to find water, because all they want is a little drink.

—Ramón Gomez de la Serna

& redwings sing to announce the coming of the moon. The coming of the day. The coming of the pale green smear of morning duckweed. Redwings sing to count the time left. Because there are no cuckoos in the Lake. To satisfy a procreant urge. Redwings sing because they can see soundwaves made by their song on the November Lake in miniature ripples that pixillate reflections of conifers. To lighten things up a little, Jesus! To avoid mortal combat. To remain sane.

Redwings sing out of an ancient contractual obligation. Because Raven stole the sun. To startle frog into believing the swim meet's started. To warn any querent away from factory-made & migraine-inducing "Danishes." Redwings sing twice each day as ritual song for the ones that went before them who visit them during afternoon naps & – when the veil is thin, & the future dangerous, to remind them of the fierce redwing will inside them to carry on, put aside petty personal redwing politics & sing as their papa taught 'em, as if there'll be no singing tomorrow & only the sounds of doors slamming shut or endless chain-sawing or rainrainrain or worse.

Redwing's song can be translated to mean: *Hallelujah! Another day in paradise! Did you see that stunning wall of stars last night? What's for breakfast? Who was that startled the buck yesterday? Where's coyote? Where's cougar? Here come the shadows. Thanks.*

Redwings sing because that's how a yogi w/ a red spot on a black wing demonstrates the loss of self-preoccupation & the assumption of responsibility for all living things in the Net of Indra. How howling autonomy manifests in the late November Redwood afternoon.

Redwing blackbirds stop singing.
How silent the eternal
Redwood
night

5:48p – N.9.13
The Lake
Loleta, CA

99. Dragon-Necked Hallucination

Smoke is the fire's conjuring trick.

—Ramón Gomez de la Serna

& the whole time he had a dragon around his neck (he wanted to *inhale* fire as well as exhale without burning his tongue, lungs & arsenal) & he'd revisit each of his 99 lives: bluesman, balladeer & barbituratist, find the clear white ashes of what they left: *the nerve that carries the load of reaction to beauty,* seeds inside the dogwood berry, astronauts in a dream (impervious to villainous freight trains) & the chance to sacrifice an eye.

& even w/ dragonfly urging him on in the eternal November Redwood afternoon he cdn't figure if dragon were blood or come, giver of form or taker of soup. & he'd petition Odin w/ thunderbolts of his own grunting &'d forego seduction as the means for swindling the mead of poetry. Wd settle for a mere murmur, a song that some'd call a *stumble.* Well pilgrims, we've hit on the dilemma. & while there'll be woodfrogs, fat California bug-fed woodfrogs, there'd be no L U N G drugs nor work, nor rent money & in their place the inner eye in focus (sometimes. Not unlike the feeling of joy in the room & feeling as groom to the eternal witch that runs things. Good witch.) There'd be

higher doses only now matcha & puer, a little more fat on the bone, gray ear whiskers & more shit-filled diapers. The coffee mug brain dent hangover remained as a migraine & the rage? The rage'd lose some of its foam to a few more malas palabras y real herbs (lavender & rosemary) & zinneas, more sunflowers & the growth of a tranquil beak as in Graves '68 *Light,* human-eyed w/ enough meat to satisfy.

Cats get nine lives & how long the life of your typical dragonfly? He'd petition Mercury & the sphere of Hod in the Kabbalah. He'd stop the boast, the teasing of table-mates at the feast & find the aid of a couple of willing Ravens who, too, knew well enough to stifle when the redwings have the stage. & figure out how to squish seventeen years into four neo-barroco paragraphs. In the end

> he'll take that black
>> Stetson & oak
>>> walking stick

111

into the rain & feel each raindrop
   (like us all, as only)
                        a reflection
                        of a reflection
                        of a reflection
                        of a reflection
                        of a...

12:15p – N.10.13
The Lake
Loleta, CA

Notes on Poems

2. Duende's Dancestep
   Quote from Lissa Wolsak

4. Angel Hack
   Nafsu: The Indonesian dictionary definition of this very common
   word is "natural appetite or desire". In Subud parlance it refers to
   "lower forces."

5. Carbonism:
   http://www.washingtonpost.com/wp–dyn/content/
   article/2010/12/02/AR2010120203102.html

6. Echoes:
   http://en.wikipedia.org/wiki/Salients

7. Winter Solstice Lunar Eclipse
   http://www.seattlepi.com/national/432071_earth19.html

9. Ancestor (Dream) Dirt
   Quotes from Nate Mackey.
   Worm courtesy of William Blake, *The Sick Rose*

10. Rivers
    http://www.todaysthv.com/news/local/story.aspx?storyid=
    137071&provider=top

    *The primary runway at the (Tampa) airport is designated 18R/36L, which means
    the runway is aligned along 180 degrees from north (that is, due south) when
    approached from the north and 360 degrees from north when approached from the
    south. Now the Federal Aviation Administration (FAA) has requested the designation
    be changed to 19R/1L to account for the movement of the magnetic north pole.*

11. Charioteering
    In Buddhist phenomenology skandhas (Sanskrit, aggregates in
    English) are any of five types of phenomena that serve as objects of
    clinging and bases for a sense of self.

13. Free Egypt

As a verb "crack", dating back to the 15th century, was to praise or boast. If you "cracked up" something you sang its praises. Therefore something that is "not all it's cracked up to be" is something that is not as good as you were told. http://www.joe-ks.com/phrases/phrasesN.htm

15. Tongues & Mirrors

Quote from Michael McClure.
Kihlguulins – The one with the beautiful voice.

16. Suicide Flowers

Hobo code images: cat = "Kind lady lives here." Plus with smile = "Doctor here, won't charge."

17. Black Sounds

Quote from Federíco Garcia Lorca.
Hobo code images: 2/10 = "There are thieves about." Three diagonal lines = "This is not a safe space."

18. Noosphere Wormride

Proportionlessness via McClure's
3.22.11 email and quotes from
The Flower Ornament Scripture
Hobo code images: Diamond plus tail: "Hold your tongue." Two parallel lines: "The sky is the limit."

19. Bendigas de Bloodhawk

S?ayahus: a horned snake in local Salish parlance who lives at Lake Xacuabš on the west bank opposite the north end of Mercer Island. Hobo code image: "A beating awaits you here."

20. Gardenspace & Hawktime

Hobo code image: "Be prepared to defend yourself."

21. Fog Drip (The Age of Veil Lifting)

Hobo code image: "Doctor Here Won't Charge."

26. Wind in the Stetsons

Hobo code image: "Officer of the Law Lives Here."

28. The Cruel Majority (After Jerome Rothenberg)
   http://www.youtube.com/watch?v=tj5uvC9cLO4

29. Into the Eight Directions (Octopus Mom)
   http://seattletimes.nwsource.com/html/fieldnotes/2015374366_
   video_eight-armed_moms_give_their_all_in_puget_sound.html

30. The Day the Weather Decided to Die
   Published in *Make It True: Poetry From Cascadia*. Won Robin Blaser
   Award, 2013, The Capilano Review. Judge, George Bowering

31. Dragonfly Resurrection
   http://seattletimes.nwsource.com/html/localnews/2015387489_
   solstice22m.html

32. Bear Camp Road
   http://en.wikipedia.org/wiki/Bear_Camp_Road

37. Power of the Pocket Journal
   Rune image – Dagaz

38. The Barking of the Bitches
   Rune image – Uruz
   Quote from psychic named *Raven*

40. Mobocracy 101
   Rune image – Nauthiz

41. Othila's New Muscle
   After "Common Thread" – Susan Point, 2000
   Quote from an email from Michael McClure

43. Wheel (Whorl)
   (After Susan Point: Looking Forward, 2000)
   Darshan, according to Hindu culture, is an act of seeing the deity
   and refers to an intense participatory relationship with art that goes
   beyond using one's eyes but is a "dynamic act of awareness" according
   to art historian Vidya Dehejia.

44. Stellar (Ella)
No podemos hacerlo sin Ella is Spanish for "we can't do it without her."

45. Cat Screams
Rune image – Berkana
Quotes from Walt Whitman, *Song of Myself*, verse 25.

46. Wolf Ride
Rune image – Algiz
http://runesecrets.com/rune-meanings/algiz
http://www.mailtribune.com/apps/pbcs.dll/article?AID=/20111106/
NEWS/111060346/-1/NEWSMAP

47. Occupy, Farewell, Spit
First quote, a favorite saying of Paul E Nelson, Sr.
http://www.angelfire.com/bc2/bluephoenixrunes/RUNES/KANO.
html
Robin Blaser quotes from page 14, Pell Mell, Coach House Press,
1988.
Rune, Kano

48. Torquemada's Revenge
http://en.wikipedia.org/wiki/Fusang
Mario Savio http://www.nytimes.com/2011/11/20/opinion/sunday/
at-occupy-berkeley-beat-poets-has-new-meaning.html

49. 49th Parallel Blues
Rune image – Algiz Reversed.

50. Nevermind Gray Waves
Rune image – Wunjo.

51. Echo in Licton Springs
http://en.wikipedia.org/wiki/Licton_Springs,_Seattle
Rune Image – Thurisaz.

53. Nothing Death
Rune Image – Fehu Reversed.

55. Graphic for *Fear is Salty.*

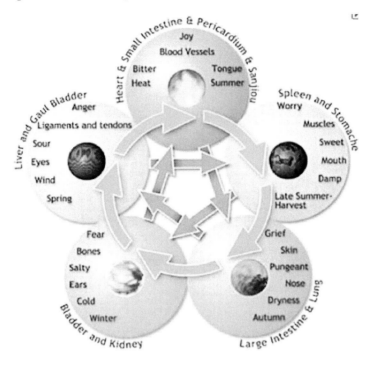

Joy
Blood Vessels
Heart & Small Intestine & Pericardium & Sanjiao
Bitter   Tongue
Heat   Summer

Spleen and Stomache
Worry
Muscles
Sweet
Mouth
Damp
Late Summer-Harvest

Liver and Gaul Bladder
Anger
Ligaments and tendons
Sour
Eyes
Wind
Spring

Fear
Bones
Salty
Ears
Cold
Winter
Bladder and Kidney

Grief
Skin
Pungeant
Nose
Dryness
Autumn
Large Intestine & Lung

56. Shooting Starward
 Quotes 1 & 3, Richard Katz, *The Science of Flower Essence Therapy.*
 Quote 2, Phyllis Baker *The Slippery Soapbox: Aphorisms and Rants.*
 Quote 4, Joe Chiveney, Aaron Kokorowski from an Exquisite Corpse
 written in a workshop at the Richard Hugo House.

57. Frog Song
 After Susan Point's *Nowhere Left.* 2000
 http://www.mister-toad.com/PacificTreeFrog.html

 Ghetto – 1605-15;<Italian, orig. the name of an island near Venice
 where Jews were forced to reside in the 16th century < Venetian,
 literally, foundry for artillery (giving the island its name), noun
 derivative of ghettare to throw < Vulgar Latin *jectāre; see jet1

61. Meat Again
 Rune image – Raido

64. Sin Malicia

Quote from *The Flower Ornament Scripture,* Vol. One, Thomas Cleary.

65. Dirty Raven Light Thief

Sophie Charlotte von Mecklenburg-Strelitz is the woman after whom the Queen Charlotte Islands (Haida Gwaii) were named.

Quote from Claude Levi-Strauss *The Raven Steals the Light*

66. Doors of Liberation

Quotes from The Flower Ornament Scripture, translated by Thomas Cleary.

68. Sowilo-Tinted Vision Field

Rune image: Sowilo

69. Go Dolly Go

Rune image: Kano

http://www.nps.gov/olym/parknews/lake-aldwell-closed-to-public-use.htm

http://en.wikipedia.org/wiki/Dolly_Varden_trout

70. The Return of the Elwha King

Rune image: Kano

http://o.seattletimes.nwsource.com/html/fieldnotes/2018961159_chinook_return_to_the_elwha.html

http://crosscut.com/2012/08/22/climate/110118/world-according-gallup-and-according-planet/

71. The Ambassador From Bakersfield

Quotes taken from *Robert Duncan: The Ambassador from Venus,* by Lisa Jarnot.

72. Moss Spruce Cedar Cathedral

Inspired by the art work of Richard Shorty and a visit to the grave of Chief Seattle.

73. Ode to Sun Mask

Inspired by the art work of Bill Henderson (Sun Mask) and Lester Bowie's *Rios Negros.*

74. The Use of Wunjo
   Quotes from *Taking Up The Runes*, Diana L. Paxson.

75. Translating the Digital Fire
   http://o.seattletimes.nwsource.com/html/localnews/2019600636_
   octo04m.html

77. Clean Shirt (It Never Entered My Mind)
   First quote from T.P. Kasulis "Zen Action, Zen Person."
   Dogen quote from "The Zen Poetry of Dogen" (Ed: Steven Heine).
   Last quote from the song "It Never Entered My Mind," lyric by
   Lorenz Hart.

78. Wren & Whale Surrender
   All quotes from *Tsawalk: A Nuu-chah-nulth Worldview* by *Umeek*, E.
   Richard Atleo.
   Tsawalk is the Nuu-chah-nulth wordldview which unifies the
   spiritual and physical.

79. Kano and The Snake
   Quote from: http://runesecrets.com/rune-meanings/kenaz

81. Moonbank (After Xi Chuan)
   Quote from Barry McKinnon: http://www.fillingstation.ca/
   news/2013/1/20/short-interview-barry-mckinnon-2

83. Buddha Diet
   Quotes from the Flower Ornament Scripture or Beck.

84. Hold the House Sparrow
   Quote: W.L. Dawson, *Birds of Ohio*, 1903.85. Soul's Same Ol' (Over
   n Over)
   1st quote: From postcard poem #396. to Dheepikaa
   Balasubramanian, Chennai, India – *Indigent Petition*.
   2nd quote: Bapak, Nov 9, 1980, Cilandak.
   3rd quote: Lonnie Hillyer on Walter Davis Jr.

86. Paulownia Tomentosa
   Quote about the newcomer from the *Seattle Times*.

88. Lesser Quantico

Quotes from *The Practice of Outside,* Robin Blaser or (quote # 2) *The Flower Ornament Scripture* (p 89,90).

89. Pocket Fetch

Quote from: http://runesecrets.com/rune-meanings/ehwaz

91. Berber City Poems

Quote from José Lezama Lima.

92. Galactic Circuit

Italics = lines taken from poems from 9.27.13 Open Books reading. Quotations are taken from extemporaneous talk between poems.

93. The Fog Wet Web

Quote from http://cliffmass.blogspot.com/2013/10/fogmageddon. html

94. Dilettante Periphery

Quotes:

1) Morris Graves
2) Claude Monet
3) Guy Anderson to Morris Graves in a 1957 letter
4) Morris Graves in a 1958 letter
5) Brenda Hillman

95. Sending Out Tendrils

Quotes:

1) Old County Cork woman attributed by Morris Graves.
2) Illustrated Encyclopaedia of Traditional Symbols.
3 & 4) Morris Graves.

96. The Gift

Written in part after the Lawrence Paul Yuxweluptun painting referenced in the poem.

97. Clues from Hell

All quotes from Morris Graves.

99. Dragon-Necked Hallucination
Quote from Morris Graves, from a Nov 1, 1948 letter. Image, Fehu